GREAT AUTHORS OF
SCIENCE FICTION
& FANTASY

Essential Authors
for Children & Teens

GREAT AUTHORS OF
SCIENCE FICTION
& FANTASY

EDITED BY JEANNE NAGLE

Britannica®
Educational Publishing

IN ASSOCIATION WITH

ROSEN
EDUCATIONAL SERVICES

Published in 2014 by Britannica Educational Publishing
(a trademark of Encyclopædia Britannica, Inc.) in association with The Rosen Publishing Group, Inc.
29 East 21st Street, New York, NY 10010.

Distributed exclusively by Rosen Publishing.
For a listing of additional Britannica Educational Publishing titles go to rosenpublishing.com.

First Edition

Britannica Educational Publishing
J.E. Luebering: Director, Core Reference Group
Anthony L. Green: Editor, Compton's by Britannica

Rosen Educational Services
Jeanne Nagle: Senior Editor
Nelson Sá: Art Director
Cindy Reiman: Photography Manager
Nicole Baker: Photo Researcher
Brian Garvey: Designer, Cover Design
Introduction and supplementary material by Joe Greek

Library of Congress Cataloging-in-Publication Data

Great authors of science fiction & fantasy/editor, Jeanne Nagle.—First edition.
    pages cm.—(Essential Authors for Children & Teens)
Includes bibliographical references and index.
ISBN 978-1-62275-090-0 (library binding)
1. Science fiction—History and criticism—Juvenile literature. 2. Fantasy fiction—History and
criticism—Juvenile literature. I. Nagle, Jeanne, editor of compilation.
PN3433.5.G74 2014
809.3'8762—dc23

2013023094

Manufactured in the United States of America

Contents

24

36

48

Introduction

All fiction authors rely on the power of the imagination, but perhaps none more so than those who write science fiction and fantasy. It is in their writings that the improbable and the seemingly impossible come together to form entirely new worlds and galaxies of colorful characters that defy reality as readers know it. The biographies of authors in this book highlight how some of the best writers in these genres accomplish this feat.

During the first half of the 20th century, fantasy fiction began reaching large audiences as a result of mass-produced "pulp" novels and magazines. Featured in these stories were memorable characters such as Robert E. Howard's Conan the Barbarian, as well as Edgar Rice Burrough's Tarzan and John Carter—all of whom have frequently returned to popularity in the form of comic books, films, and cartoons that continue to entertain new generations of fantasy fans.

By the 1950s, longer novels in the genre, such as J.R.R. Tolkein's *The*

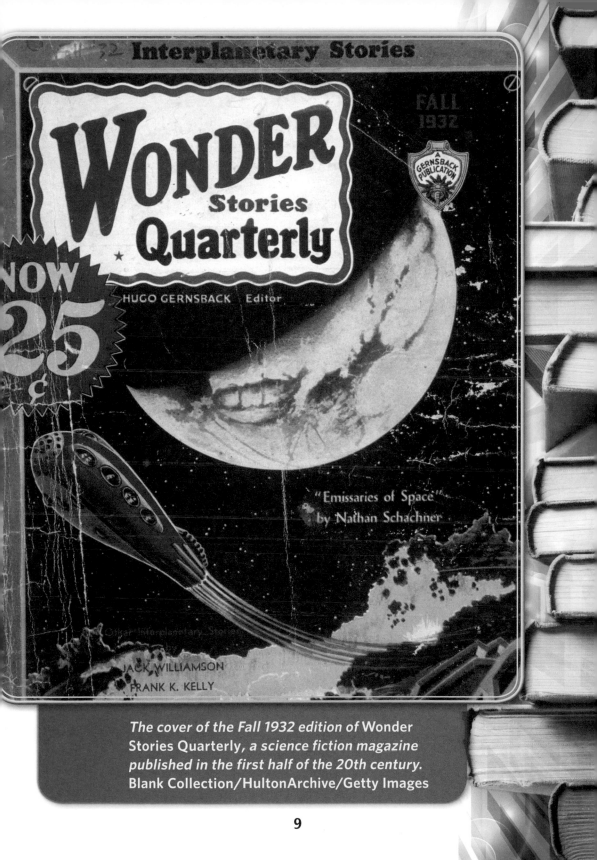

The cover of the Fall 1932 edition of Wonder Stories Quarterly, a science fiction magazine published in the first half of the 20th century.
Blank Collection/HultonArchive/Getty Images

Lord of the Rings trilogy and C.S. Lewis's *The Chronicles of Narnia*, formed the foundation for what is considered modern fantasy, which utilizes magic and mythical creatures such as elves and gnomes. Such elements remain within the genre, as proven by the wildly popular *Harry Potter* series by J.K. Rowling and the *Game of Thrones* series by George R.R. Martin.

Whereas fantasy is rooted firmly in the realm of imagination, science fiction often combines elements of scientific theory, law, and technological progress to transport readers to undiscovered worlds. Many of the sci fi writers featured in this book have been considered visionaries because the theoretical (in theory only) elements of their stories would later become reality. For example, the early submarine designer Simon Lake praised Jules Verne's 1870 novel *20,000 Leagues Under the Sea* as an inspiration behind much of his work.

Between 1938 and 1946, a period known as the "Golden Age" of science fiction, writers veered away from fantasy elements and began focusing on known and theorized scientific and technological concepts. Many of the best known and respected writers of "hard sci fi" emerged during this period, including Arthur C. Clark, Philip K. Dick, and Robert A. Heinlein. Even more writers in the genre were guided in their work by the influential editor and writer John W. Campbell.

Later, authors such as Anthony Burgess, Ray Bradbury, and Isaac Asimov began to focus on the human element and the societal implications of technological progress. Asimov in particular viewed sci fi as "the branch of literature which deals with the response of human beings to changes in the level of science and technology"—a statement that is clearly demonstrated throughout his epic *Foundation* series.

The authors profiled in this book have invited generations of readers to look beyond the only world they know and consider what is possible. As such, their contributions to literature and society in general are invaluable.

DOUGLAS ADAMS

(b. 1952–d. 2001)

Douglas Adams was a British comic writer whose works satirize contemporary life through a luckless main character who deals with societal forces beyond his control. Adams is best known for the mock science fiction series known collectively as *The Hitchhiker's Guide to the Galaxy.*

Douglas Noël Adams was born March 11, 1952, in Cambridge, Eng. He received an M.A. (1974) in English literature from the University of Cambridge, where he wrote comedy sketches for the performing arts society. He was a writer and script editor for the television series *Doctor Who* and wrote scripts for the British Broadcasting Corporation from 1978 to 1980.

The Hitchhiker's Guide series is a parody that pokes fun at modern society with biting humor and pessimism. The work achieved great popularity, first as a twelve-part series on the radio in 1978–80 and then in a five-book series that sold more than 14 million copies internationally. The books in the series are *The Hitchhiker's Guide to the Galaxy* (1979), *The Restaurant*

Douglas Adams, at his Santa Barbara, Calif., home in 2000. Dan Callister/Getty Images

at the End of the Universe (1980), *Life, the Universe and Everything* (1982), *So Long, and Thanks for All the Fish* (1985), and *Mostly Harmless* (1992). *The Hitchhiker's Guide* was adapted for television, theater, and film, and was used as the basis of an interactive computer program.

Adams satirized the detective-story genre with *Dirk Gently's Holistic Detective*

Agency (1987) and *The Long Dark Tea-Time of the Soul* (1988). Other works include The *Meaning of Liff* (with John Lloyd; 1983), *The Utterly Utterly Merry Comic Relief Christmas Book* (coeditor, with Peter Fincham; 1986), and *Last Chance to See...* (with Mark Carwardine; 1990), a radio series also published in 1990 as a nonfiction book.

Adams died of a heart attack on May 11, 2001, in Montecito, Calif. He was forty-nine years old.

BRIAN ALDISS

(b. 1925–)

By the end of the twentieth century, Brian Aldiss was considered the elder statesman of British science fiction writers. A prolific author of science fiction short stories and novels that display great range in style and approach, Aldiss wrote mainstream fiction, essays, and literary criticism as well.

Brian Wilson Aldiss was born on Aug. 18, 1925, in East Dereham, Norfolk, Eng., the son of a department store owner. He

spent his formative years growing up in the rural areas of Devon and Norfolk, receiving his education at Framlingham College in Suffolk and the West Buckland School in Devon. He served with the British Army in Southeast Asia from 1944 to 1947, gaining experiences that later would provide material for many of his stories. After his discharge from the army in 1947, Aldiss found work as a bookseller in Oxford. He spent the next nine years working full-time in bookstores while writing on the side. His first two professional sales, an article entitled "A Book in Time" that appeared in *The Bookseller* and a science fiction short story ("Criminal Record," published in the magazine *Science Fantasy*) appeared in 1954.

After the successful publication of his first novel, *The Brightfount Diaries* (1955), Aldiss left bookselling in 1956 to write full-time. His next book was a science fiction novel, *Non-Stop* (1958). Aldiss went on to write more than forty science fiction novels and short-story collections. He showed great versatility in his explorations of the genre's classic themes and premises, while also maintaining an

Science fiction writer Brian Aldiss. Writer Pictures/
Geraint Lewis/AP Images

interest in human character. Many collections of his stories are available, including *Best Science Fiction Stories of Brian W. Aldiss* (1965) and *A Brian Aldiss Omnibus* (1969 and 1971). Outstanding individual volumes of his stories include *The Canopy of Time* (1959), *Hothouse* (1962), *Starswarm* (1964), and *The Saliva Tree* (1966). Another book, *Frankenstein Unbound* (1973), was made into a movie by Roger Corman in 1990.

Aldiss was also an influential editor of numerous anthologies of science fiction. In addition, he wrote criticism, essays, travelogues, and autobiographical novels. His later fiction includes *Moreau's Other Island* (1980); the three novels of his ambitious *Helliconia Trilogy* (1982–85), which chronicles life and human civilization on a planet where each season lasts for centuries; and *White Mars: Or, The Mind Set Free: A 21st-Century Utopia* (1999). After his autobiography (*The Twinkling of an Eye: Or, My Life as an Englishman*) was published in 1998, Aldiss wrote a book about how he and his wife dealt with her terminal illness (*When the Feast Is Finished*, 1999). The recipient of countless awards and honors during his career, Aldiss was elected

a Grand Master by the Science Fiction Writers of America in 2000.

LLOYD ALEXANDER

(b. 1924–d. 2007)

With lively novels and picture books that take characters through exciting physical and personal journeys, U.S. author Lloyd Alexander has attracted attention from both critics and young readers, especially those interested in the fantasy genre.

Alexander was born on Jan. 30, 1924, in Philadelphia, Pa. He was an avid reader throughout his childhood and especially enjoyed fairy tales and mythology. After high school, he became a bank messenger and wrote in his free time. He briefly took writing classes at a local college before joining the United States Army in 1943 with hopes that military adventures would make him a better writer. Following his discharge in 1946, he attended the Sorbonne in France.

Alexander translated several books from French into English, edited an

industrial magazine, and wrote advertising copy in the United States in the late 1940s and early 1950s while trying to get published. He first found success with *And Let the Credit Go* (1955), one of several adult books based on his own experiences. He eventually turned his efforts toward children's literature and released his first juvenile fantasy, *Time Cat: The Remarkable Journeys of Jason and Gareth*, in 1963.

The Book of Three (1964) launched a five-book series chronicling the rise of a young hero named Taran from an assistant pig keeper to leader of the imaginary kingdom of Prydain. Along the way, Taran and his memorable companions confront villains, war, and personal dilemmas. The second novel in the series, *The Black Cauldron* (1965), was chosen as a Newbery Honor Book in 1966, and the last installment, *The High King* (1968), won the Newbery Medal in 1969. The series also includes *The Castle of Llyr* (1966) and *Taran Wanderer* (1967). The animated Disney feature film *The Black Cauldron* (1985) was based on the Prydain novels.

Alexander also penned the *Westmark* trilogy and the *Vesper Holly* adventures.

Westmark (1981), *The Kestrel* (1982), and *The Beggar Queen* (1984) deal with concepts such as democracy, freedom, and corruption in stories about the political struggles of the fictional kingdom of Westmark. Books starring spirited 19th-century orphan Vesper Holly and her guardian offer fast-paced journeys through distant lands where the two characters help right injustices. The series includes *The Illyrian Adventure* (1986), *The Drackenberg Adventure* (1988), and others.

Alexander received many honors, including the National Book Award in 1971 for *The Marvelous Misadventures of Sebastian* (1970), the American Book Award in 1982 for *Westmark*, the Austrian Children's Book Award in 1984 for *The First Two Lives of Lukas-Kasha* (1978), and the *Boston Globe–Horn Book* Award for Picture Books in 1993 for *The Fortune-tellers* (1992). For his overall contribution to children's literature, he received the 1986 Regina Medal. In addition to writing, Alexander served on the editorial board of the children's magazine *Cricket* and served as an author-in-residence at various Pennsylvania schools. He died on May 17, 2007, in Drexel Hill, Pa.

POUL ANDERSON

(b. 1926–d. 2001)

P oul Anderson was a prolific American writer of science fiction and fantasy. He has often been praised for his scrupulous attention to scientific detail.

Poul William Anderson was born in Bristol, Pa., on Nov. 25, 1926. He published his first science fiction story while an undergraduate at the University of Minnesota and became a freelance writer following his graduation with a degree in physics in 1948. He published his first novel, *Vault of the Ages*, in 1952 and thereafter produced several books each year. A number of his works concern the "future history" of what he called the Technic Civilization, an age of human history lasting from the years 2100 to 7100. Much of the content of these books, such as *Agent of the Terran Empire* (1965), is patterned after events that occurred during the European Age of Exploration.

In *Tau Zero* (1970), Anderson centered the action within a spaceship, the speed of which is approaching the speed of light. Inside, the travelers experience time as they have always known it while witnessing through the portholes the collapse and rebirth of the universe. Other notable books include *A Midsummer Tempest* (1974), *The Boat of a Million Years* (1989), and *Genesis* (2000), which received the John W. Campbell Award in 2001.

Just as Anderson's scientific training lends weight to his science fiction, his interest in Scandinavian languages and literature influenced many of his fantasy novels. *The Merman's Children* (1979), for example, portrays the plight of a surviving species of mermen within human society, a theme found in medieval Danish balladry.

Anderson received numerous Hugo Awards for short fiction and was a three-time recipient of the Nebula Award (1971, 1972, and 1981). In 2000 he was inducted into the Science Fiction and Fantasy Hall of Fame. He died of cancer on July 31, 2001.

ISAAC ASIMOV

(b. 1920–d. 1992)

The author of more than 400 books on a broad range of subjects, Isaac Asimov called himself a "born explainer." His

Prolific science and science fiction writer Isaac Asimov, autographing his work at a 1984 book fair in New York City. © AP Images

streamlined versions of science facts are as popular as his science fiction, and his works include history and mysteries.

Asimov was born in Petrovichi, Russia, on Jan. 2, 1920. His family moved to the United States when he was three. When he was about nine, he began reading the science fiction magazines stocked in his parents' candy store in Brooklyn, N.Y. In 1938, while he was still a teenager, he sold his first short story, "Marooned Off Vesta," to *Amazing Stories*.

After postgraduate work at Columbia University, Asimov began teaching biochemistry at Boston University in 1949. The next year his first books—the futuristic satire *Pebble in the Sky* and the thriller *I, Robot*—were published. As the pace and scope of his writing increased, he moved to New York City for a freelance career but retained his academic title.

Decades ahead of their time, Asimov's *The Intelligent Man's Guide to Science* (1960) and *Today and Tomorrow and ...* (1973) are still popular with researchers. With his wife, Janet, he wrote a series of children's books about a mixed-up robot named Norby. Two volumes of autobiography—*In Memory Yet Green* and *In Joy Still Felt*—cover the years 1920 to 1954 and 1954 to 1978.

The more than thirty subjects in Asimov's *How Did We Find Out* series

range from numbers (1973) to photosynthesis and microwaves (both 1989). Other subjects in the young people's series are dinosaurs, germs, volcanoes, DNA, and the brain. In 1989 he also published the novel *Nemesis*; *SciQuest* selections, *The Tyrannosaurus Prescription and 100 Other Essays*; and *Asimov on Science*, a collection of *Fantasy and Science Fiction* columns written over a thirty-year period. He died in New York City on Apr. 6, 1992.

J.G. BALLARD

(b. 1930–d. 2009)

The works of British author J.G. Ballard are set in ecologically unbalanced landscapes caused by technological excess. His stories are often surreal and frequently violent.

James Graham Ballard was born in Shanghai, China, on November 15, 1930. The son of a British business executive based in China, he spent four years of his boyhood in a Japanese prison camp near Shanghai during World War II. This experience is recounted in his largely autobiographical novel *Empire of the Sun* (1984; film 1987). The devastated city and nearby countryside also provided settings for several of his apocalyptic novels.

He later attended King's College, Cambridge, but left without a degree. His first short stories appeared in the 1950s. Beginning in the 1960s, Ballard wrote longer

Author J.G. Ballard, relaxing at his home in England.
Writer Pictures/John Lawerence/AP Images

works, including *The Drowned World* (1962), *The Wind from Nowhere* (1962), *The Burning World* (1964), and *The Crystal World* (1966).

In 1970, Ballard published *The Atrocity Exhibition*, a collection of short stories filled with gory images. He followed that with several apocalyptic novels, which depicted middle-class people becoming savages. These works include *Crash* (1973; film 1996), *Concrete Island* (1974), and *High Rise* (1975).

In contrast to the bleak future depicted in his apocalyptic novels, Ballard also wrote short stories that have been described as almost wistful. His short-story collection *Vermilion Sands* (1971) describes a technologically advanced resort community where the population's every desire is met, while the stories in *War Fever* (1990) are tinged with humor.

Other works by Ballard include *The Day of Creation* (1987), *The Kindness of Women* (1991), *Rushing to Paradise* (1994), *Cocaine Nights* (1996), *Super-Cannes* (2000), *Millennium People* (2003), and *Kingdom Come* (2006). His essays and reviews were compiled in *A User's Guide to the Millennium* (1996), and *The Complete Short Stories of J.G. Ballard* was released in two volumes in 2006. An autobiography, *Miracles of Life*, was published in 2008. Ballard died in London on April 19, 2009.

ALFRED BESTER

(b. 1913–d. 1987)

A lfred Bester was an innovative American science fiction writer. Though his literary output was comparatively small, his work was highly influential. His fiction often employed narrative techniques, such as interior monologue and deep characterization, that were new to the science fiction genre.

Born in New York, N.Y., Bester attended the University of Pennsylvania, from which he received his bachelor's degree in 1935. From 1939 to 1942 he published fourteen short stories in science fiction magazines. Among these early stories was "Hell Is Forever" (1942), which, in its fast pacing and obsessive characters, anticipated the style of his major novels. After 1942 he wrote scenarios for superhero comic books and scripts for radio and television. During this time he also created English-language librettos for operas by the classical composers Giuseppe Verdi and Modest Moussorgsky.

Bester's first novel was the satiric non–science fiction work *Who He?* (1953), but his first major work was the novel *The*

Demolished Man (1953). He followed that with *Tiger! Tiger!* (1956; also published as *The Stars My Destination*). He subsequently published several short-story collections, including *Starburst* (1958) and *The Dark Side of the Earth* (1964).

During the 1960s and early '70s, Bester was a writer for and then editor of the travel magazine *Holiday*, which left him little time for his own writing; he returned to science fiction when *Holiday* ceased publication. Among his later works are *The Computer Connection* (1975; also published as *Extro*), *Golem* [100] (1980) and *The Deceivers* (1982). Bester died in Doylestown, Pa., in October of 1987.

JAMES BLISH

(b. 1921–d. 1975)

James Blish was an author and critic of science fiction who was best known for the *Cities in Flight* series (1950–62) and the novel *A Case of Conscience* (1958). His work, which often examined philosophical ideas, was part of the more sophisticated science fiction that arose in the 1950s.

Born in East Orange, N.J., James Benjamin Blish had been a fan of science fiction since his childhood. His first short story, "Emergency Refueling," was published in the magazine *Super Science Stories* in 1940. After receiving a bachelor's degree in zoology from Rutgers University in 1942, Blish served in the U.S. Army from 1942 to 1944. After his discharge he attended graduate school at Columbia University but left in 1946 without completing a degree. He worked mainly in public relations writing advertising copy until 1968, when he was able to turn to fiction writing full-time.

Beginning in 1950, Blish wrote the short stories that became the first published novel of the *Cities in Flight* series, *Earthman, Come Home* (1955). The story is set in New York City, which travels among the stars using an anti-gravity drive, the "spindizzy." A prequel, *They Shall Have Stars* (1956), is about the invention of the spindizzy amid the decline of Western civilization in the early twenty-first century. A new interstellar civilization emerges in *A Life for the Stars* (1962) when Earth's cities use the spindizzies to escape their home planet. The series culminates in *The Triumph of Time* (1958) with the end of the universe and the birth of new universes in 4004.

Blish's novel *A Case of Conscience* won the Hugo Award for best novel in 1959. The work was part of a thematically connected series called *After Such Knowledge*. The other novels in the series included *Doctor Mirabilis* (1964) and two novels that Blish considered as one work: *Black Easter: Or, Faust Aleph-Null* (1968) and *The Day After Judgement* (1971), a fantasy in which Satan and his demons conquer Earth.

Blish was also one of the first critics of science fiction, and he judged it by the standards applied to "serious" literature. He took to task his fellow authors for such deficiencies as bad grammar and the misunderstanding of scientific concepts, and chided the magazine editors who accepted and published such poor material without editorial intervention. Much of his criticism was published in "fanzines" (amateur publications written by science fiction fans) in the 1950s under the pseudonym William Atheling, Jr., and was collected in *The Issue at Hand* (1964) and *More Issues at Hand* (1970).

Blish moved to England in 1969. Much of the remainder of his career was devoted to writing twelve collections of short stories based on the episodes of the American

television series *Star Trek*, which Blish felt had greatly expanded the audience for science fiction. He died in Henley-on-Thames, Oxfordshire, Eng., in 1975.

BEN BOVA

(b. 1932–)

Ben Bova began writing his first science fiction novel during the early years of the Cold War, when he was seventeen. The story, revolving around a race to the Moon between the Soviet Union and the United States, received positive feedback for its literary style but remained unpublished. One publisher told Bova that no one would touch the book because of concerns there would be backlash from the U.S. government for entertaining the idea that the Soviets could send a human into outer space before the Americans could do so. This was in the 1950s—only a handful of years before Soviet cosmonaut Yuri Gagarin became the first person in space, in 1961.

Born in Philadelphia, Pa., on Nov. 8, 1932, Benjamin William Bova spent several years working as a newspaper reporter

before eventually being hired in 1956 as a technical writer for Project Vanguard, the first American artificial satellite program. His first published novel, *The Star Conquerers* (1959), was released shortly before he took a marketing position with Avco Everett Research Laboratory. While working at Avco throughout the 1960s, he had the opportunity to engage with leading scientists in emerging fields such as high-powered lasers, plasma dynamics, and artificial hearts—concepts that he would later incorporate into his writing.

Bova went on to write more than 120 science fact and fiction books over his career. Many of his fiction works, including *Privateers* (1985) and *Jupiter* (2000), focused on human colonization of the universe and the underlying notion that governments are incapable of accomplishing such feats.

Bova was also an accomplished editor throughout the 1970s and early 1980s. He won the Hugo Award for best editor (short form) six times while working for *Analog Science Fiction* magazine and also served as the editor of *Omni* magazine for four years. During his tenure at both publications, Bova also wrote and published several anthologies.

In the 1990s and into the twenty-first century, Bova wrote several novels that were to become part of his *Grand Tour* collection of books about colonization throughout the distant reaches of the solar system. The series includes *Titan* (2006), which won the John W. Campbell Memorial Award in 2007. In 2008, Bova was awarded the Robert A. Heinlein Award for his works and contributions to literature.

RAY BRADBURY

(b. 1920–d. 2012)

In his stories, U.S. author Ray Bradbury wove together the intrigue of changing technology with insightful social commentary. One of his best-known works was *The Martian Chronicles* (1950), a collection of interrelated stories concerning colonization of the planet Mars that attracted readers both young and old. In it, Bradbury portrayed the strengths and weaknesses of human beings as they encountered a new world.

Ray Douglas Bradbury was born on August 22, 1920, in Waukegan, Illinois. He

Ray Bradbury at a 2000 book signing in Los Angeles, Calif. Jon Kopaloff/Getty Images

grew up in Waukegan and in Los Angeles, where he founded a magazine called *Futuria Fantasia* while in high school. He sold his first short story when he was twenty-one years old. His early stories were published in pulp magazines, but Bradbury later published stories in such mainstream magazines as *The New Yorker*, *Mademoiselle*, and the *Saturday Evening Post*. His science fiction and fantasy short-story collections included *The Martian Chronicles*, *The Illustrated Man* (1951), and *Dinosaur Tales* (1983). Bradbury's 1980 collection, *The Stories of Ray Bradbury*, covers a wide range of topics, none of which is truly science fiction. His novels included *Fahrenheit 451* (1953), *Dandelion Wine* (1957), and *Something Wicked This Way Comes* (1962). *Fahrenheit 451* was made into a motion picture in 1966, and *The Martian Chronicles* later appeared both as a motion picture and a television miniseries.

In 1954 Bradbury was honored with an award from the National Institute of Arts and Letters for his contribution to American literature. In 1956 he collaborated with John Huston to create the screenplay for *Moby Dick*. In addition to fiction Bradbury wrote *Zen and the Art of Writing* (1973) and also published such dramas as *The*

Anthem Sprinters (1963), *The Wonderful Ice Cream Suit* (1965), and *The Pedestrian* (1966). His volumes of poetry included *When Elephants Last in the Dooryard Bloomed* (1972), *Where Robot Mice & Robot Men Run Around in Robot Towns* (1977), and *The Haunted Computer and the Android Pope* (1981).

Bradbury's short film *Icarus Montgolfier Wright* (1962) was nominated for an Academy Award in 1963. Bradbury also wrote for television, including eight episodes of *Alfred Hitchcock Presents*. His work was represented in hundreds of anthologies of poetry, science fiction, short stories, and American literature. Bradbury received critical praise for the precision and creativity of his writing and for the freshness of his imagery. Bradbury died on June 5, 2012, in Los Angeles, California.

MARION ZIMMER BRADLEY

(b. 1930–d. 1999)

Marion Zimmer Bradley was known especially for her *Darkover* series of

science fiction novels and for her reimaginings of Classical myths and legends from the perspective of female characters.

Born in Albany, N.Y., on June 3, 1930, Marion Zimmer studied at the New York State College for Teachers from 1946 to 1948. After her career was established, she graduated from Hardin-Simmons College in 1964. In 1949 she married Robert A. Bradley, from whom she later was divorced. She retained his name professionally.

Bradley was a prolific writer, producing numerous historical, fantasy, and gothic novels and short stories under her own name and several pseudonyms. She is, however, best known for her many science fiction novels and stories. She published her first important work, the story "Centaurus Changeling," in 1954. Her first novel, *The Door Through Space*, appeared in 1961. Two more novels, *The Sword of Aldones* and *The Planet Savers*, were published in 1962. Both take place on Darkover, a planet that is home to a lost Terran (Earth) colony. It became the setting for a series of more than twenty science fiction novels by Bradley; other writers also set their own work on Darkover.

Bradley achieved best-seller status with *The Mists of Avalon* (1982), a retelling of the Arthurian legend with an emphasis on the female characters. Similarly, *The Firebrand* (1987) reworked the *Iliad* from the perspective of the female characters. Bradley subsequently wrote several prequels to *The Mists of Avalon*, including *The Forest House* (1994) and *Lady of Avalon* (1997). In 1995 she introduced the *Light* series.

Many of Bradley's later novels were written in collaboration with other authors, notably Diana L. Paxson. Bradley also edited *Marion Zimmer Bradley's Fantasy Magazine*, which she started in 1988. She died in Berkeley, Calif., on Sept. 25, 1999.

TERRY BROOKS

(b. 1944–)

Early in his writing career, U.S. writer Terry Brooks attempted writing within several genres, including westerns and science fiction, but he failed to find his niche. It was after reading J.R.R. Tolkien's *Lord of the Rings* trilogy that Brooks realized that the fantasy genre

offered all of the elements of writing he had been seeking.

Terence Dean Brooks was born Jan. 8, 1944, in Sterling, Ill. He obtained his graduate degree from the School of Law at Washington & Lee University in Lexington, Va., and became a practicing attorney. While working as a lawyer, Brooks worked on the first three books in his *Shannara* series: *The Sword of Shannara* (1977), *The Elfstones of Shannara* (1982), and *The Wishsong of Shannara* (1985). After the success of his third book, he left his law practice to devote more of his time to writing.

Brooks found both critical and financial success again with *Magic Kindom for Sale—Sold!* (1986), for which he won the Locus Poll Award for best fantasy novel. The book marked the beginning of his *Landover* series, which follows the story of Ben Holiday, a man from Earth who holds the deed to a fantastical kingdom that he must protect from villains, such as the powerful witch Nightshade.

In his bestselling *Word and Void* trilogy—*Running with the Demon* (1997), *A Knight of the Word* (1998), and *Angel Fire East* (1999)—Brooks drew inspiration from his childhood in Illinois to create a dark

urban setting where the protagonists use magic to fend off evil forces that threaten humanity. His *Genesis of Shannara* series, concluding with *The Gypsy Morph* (1998), served as a bridge to connect the *Word and Void* trilogy to the original *Shannara* series. He would return to the *Shannara* series time and again throughout his career, eventually publishing more than twenty-five titles under that banner.

JOHN BRUNNER

(b. 1934–d. 1995)

John Brunner was one of the most revered British science fiction writers of the twentieth century. During the 1950s and early 1960s, Brunner wrote several novels and stories that centered on conventional science fiction themes such as deep-space adventures.

John Kilian Houston Brunner was born in Preston Crowmarsh, Oxfordshire, Eng., on Sept. 24, 1934. From an early age he showed a talent for writing. His first book, *Galactic Storm* (1951), was published when he was seventeen under the name Gill

Hunt—one of several pen names he used throughout his career. Beginning in 1953, he served a three-year stint as an officer in the Royal Air Force. By 1958 he was ready to focus on a full-time writing career.

Many of Brunner's earlier books, including *The Super Barbarians* (1962) and *The Astronauts Must Not Land* (1963), found relative success among readers and critics. *The Whole Man* (1964), which was nominated for a Hugo Award for Best Novel in 1965, marked a transition away from the traditional, action-focused writing of his previous stories.

Brunner's most prolific period was between 1968 and 1975, when he published a number of works, including *Stand on Zanzibar* (1968), which won the Hugo Award for Best Novel in 1969; *The Jagged Orbit* (1969); and *The Sheep Look Up* (1972). He is best remembered for *The Shockwave Rider* (1975), which is often referred to as the first cyberpunk novel, meaning it combined themes of urban cynicism—a "punk" mentality—and an increasing prevalence of advanced, futuristic technology. Confronted by the horrors of information overload, corporate domination, and a lack of privacy, the hero uses his hacking skills

to change his identity as he flees from authorities.

Brunner died on Aug. 26, 1994. He suffered a fatal stroke while attending the 53rd World Science Fiction Convention in Glasgow, Scotland.

LOIS McMASTER BUJOLD

(b. 1949–)

The winner of four Hugo Awards for best novel, science fiction and fantasy writer Lois McMaster Bujold earned critical recognition for her ability to incorporate the styles of different genres into her writing, including mystery, romance, coming-of-age, and horror. Her interest in science fiction came at an early age when she would pick up the magazines and paperbacks brought home by her father, Robert Charles McMaster.

Lois Joy McMaster was born on Nov. 2, 1949, in Columbus, Ohio. Growing up during the 1960s, she was influenced by the works of Arthur C. Clarke, Robert A.

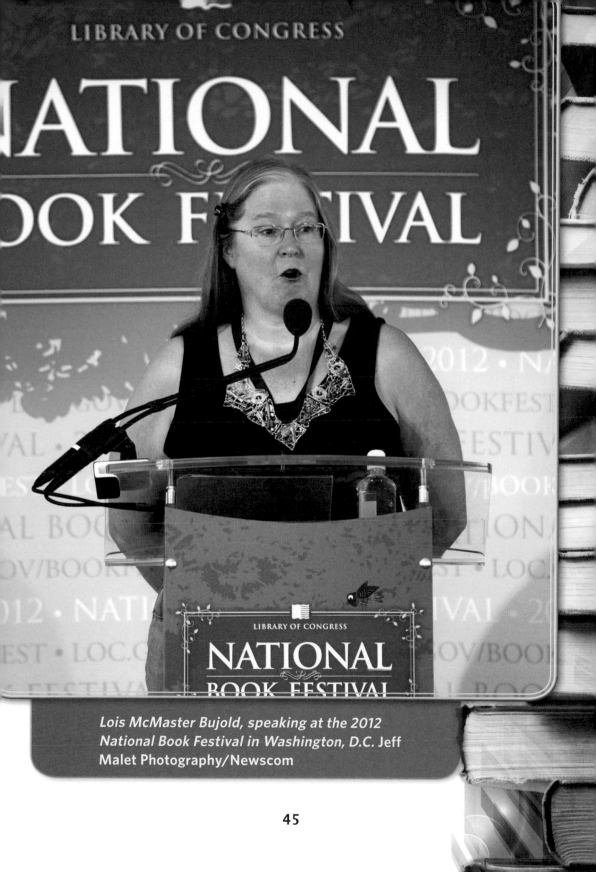

Lois McMaster Bujold, speaking at the 2012 National Book Festival in Washington, D.C. Jeff Malet Photography/Newscom

Heinlein, and Isaac Asimov—prominent writers of what is often considered the "Golden Age" of science fiction. She met and married John Bujold, who was also an avid science fiction fan.

After becoming inspired by the writing of a friend, Bujold began focusing on writing her own stories. Her first published novel, *Shards of Honor* (1986), was quickly followed by the release of *The Warrior's Apprentice* (1986) and *Ethan of Athos* (1986). The books marked the beginning of the *Vorkosigan Saga*, a critically acclaimed series of novels and short stories. She won Hugo Awards for several installments in the series, including *The Vor Game* (1990), *Barrayar* (1991), and *Mirror Dance* (1994). Bujold partially credited the story of one of the series's protagonists, Miles Vorkosigan—a man beset by physical handicaps and a drive to equal the accomplishments of his father—to the relationship she had with her own father, a renowned engineer and physicist.

At the beginning of the twenty-first century Bujold ventured into the fantasy genre, writing two series. The *Chalion* series, set within a medieval kingdom, began with *The Curse of Chalion* (2001). The second *Chalion* book, *Paladin of Souls* (2003), earned Bujold her fourth Hugo Award, matching Robert A. Heinlein's record. Bujold's third series, a crossover between fantasy and romance, is known as the *Sharing Knife*, which began with *Beguilement* (2006) and concluded with *Horizon* (2009).

ANTHONY BURGESS

(b. 1917–d. 1993)

The British novelist, critic, and man of letters Anthony Burgess worked in a number of disciplines—fiction, music, journalism, and criticism among them—and was considered one of his generation's most original writers. He wrote more than fifty books and considered himself primarily a comic writer, but he was best known for his novel *A Clockwork Orange*, which portrays a bleak, violent future in which gangs of teenagers commit acts of violence to rebel against the conformity of their society.

John Anthony Burgess Wilson was born on Feb. 25, 1917, in Manchester, Eng. He developed an interest in music at an early age, taught himself to play the piano, and,

Author Anthony Burgess, best known for penning A Clockwork Orange. *Rex Features/AP Images*

while still in school, wrote a cello concerto and a symphony. After receiving a degree in English from Manchester University in 1940, he served in the army (1940–46), taught in the extramural department of Birmingham University (1946–50), worked for the Ministry of Education (1948–50), and was English master at Banbury

Grammar School (1950–54). He then served as education officer in Malaya and Borneo (1954–59), where he wrote three novels with a Malayan setting.

After returning to England Burgess became a full-time and prolific professional writer. His novels are characterized by verbal inventiveness, erudition, sharp social satire, and a note of the bizarre. Under the name Anthony Burgess he wrote the novels *The Wanting Seed* (1962), an anti-utopian view of an overpopulated world, and *Honey for the Bears* (1963). As Joseph Kell he wrote *One Hand Clapping* (1961) and *Inside Mr. Enderby* (1963).

A Clockwork Orange (1962), which established Burgess's reputation, is written in a futuristic slang vocabulary invented by the author, in part by adaptation of Russian words. The 1971 film version of the novel, directed by Stanley Kubrick, became controversial for its violence. Other novels include *The Eve of Saint Venus* (1964) and *Enderby Outside* (1968). The latter is part of a series of humorous novels centered on the lyric poet F.X. Enderby, whom many critics have seen as a spokesman for Burgess himself. His later works include *Earthly Powers* (1980), *The End of the World News* (1983), *The*

Kingdom of the Wicked (1985), *Any Old Iron* (1989), and *A Dead Man in Deptford* (1993). He also wrote two volumes of autobiography, *Little Wilson and Big God* (1986) and *You've Had Your Time* (1990), literary criticism, and several biographies. Burgess died in London on Nov. 22, 1993.

EDGAR RICE BURROUGHS

(b. 1875–d. 1950)

The first story published by American novelist Edgar Rice Burroughs was a work of science fiction about life on Mars. However, Burroughs received enduring fame as the author of the Tarzan adventure stories. In Tarzan, he had created a folk hero known around the world.

Burroughs was born on Sept. 1, 1875, in Chicago, Ill. The son of a wealthy businessman, he was educated at private schools in Chicago, at the prestigious Phillips Academy in Andover, Massachusetts (from which he was expelled), and at Michigan Military Academy, where he subsequently taught briefly. He spent the years 1897 to 1911 in numerous unsuccessful jobs and business ventures in Chicago and Idaho. Eventually he settled in Chicago with a wife and three children.

Burroughs started his writing career producing advertising copy but then turned to fiction. His story *Under the*

Author of the Tarzan adventure series Edgar Rice Burroughs. Encyclopædia Britannica, Inc.

Moons of Mars appeared in serial form in the adventure magazine *The All-Story* in 1912. It was so successful that Burroughs turned to writing full-time. The work was later turned into a novel titled *A Princess of Mars* (1917) and was released as a film under the title *John Carter* (2012).

The first Tarzan story appeared in 1912, followed in 1914 by *Tarzan of the Apes*, the first of 25 such books in a series. The tales revolved around the son of an English nobleman abandoned in the African jungle during infancy and brought up by apes. The Tarzan stories were translated into more than fifty-six languages and were also popular in comic-strip, motion-picture, television, and radio versions.

In 1919, in order to be near the filming of his Tarzan movies, Burroughs bought an estate near Hollywood (at a site that would later be named Tarzana). He continued to write novels, ultimately publishing some sixty-eight titles in all. During World War II he became a correspondent for the *Los Angeles Times*, and at age sixty-six was the oldest war correspondent covering the South Pacific theater. Burroughs died on March 19, 1950, in Encino, Calif.

OCTAVIA E. BUTLER

(b. 1947–d. 2006)

O ctavia Butler was chiefly noted for her science fiction novels about future societies and superhuman powers. They are noteworthy for their unique synthesis of science fiction, mysticism, mythology, and African American spiritualism.

Octavia Estelle Butler was born in Pasadena, Calif., and educated at Pasadena City College (A.A., 1968), California State University, and the University of California at Los Angeles. Encouraged by Harlan Ellison, she began her writing career in 1970. The first of her novels, *Patternmaster* (1976), was the beginning of her five-volume *Patternist* series about an elite group of mentally linked telepaths ruled by Doro, a 4,000-year-old immortal African. Other novels in the series are *Mind of My Mind* (1977), *Survivor* (1978), *Wild Seed* (1980), and *Clay's Ark* (1984).

In *Kindred* (1979) a contemporary black woman is sent back in time to a pre–Civil War plantation, becomes a slave, and res-cues her white, slave-owning ancestor. Her later novels include the *Xenogenesis*

Octavia Butler, the first science fiction writer to receive a MacArthur Foundation fellowship.
Malcolm Ali/WireImage/Getty Images

trilogy—*Dawn: Xenogenesis* (1987), *Adulthood Rites* (1988), and *Imago* (1989)—and *The Parable of the Sower* (1993), *The Parable of the Talents* (1998), and *Fledgling* (2005). Butler's short story "Speech Sounds" won a Hugo Award in 1984, and her story "Bloodchild," about human male slaves who incubate their alien masters' eggs, won both Hugo and Nebula awards. Her collection *Bloodchild and Other Stories* was published in 1995. That same year Butler became the first science fiction writer to be awarded a MacArthur Foundation fellowship, and in 2000 she received a PEN Award for lifetime achievement.

Fledgling turned out to be Butler's last published work. She died on February 24, 2006, in Lake Forest Park, Wa., at age fifty-eight.

JOHN W. CAMPBELL

(b. 1910–d. 1971)

The work of American science fiction writer John W. Campbell was widely imitated. It is for this, and his successful career as a science fiction editor, that

Campbell is considered the father of modern science fiction.

John Williams Campbell was born in Newark, N.J., on June 8, 1910. He spent his childhood reading widely and experimenting with science, and he began writing science fiction while in college. His first published story, "When the Atoms Failed" (1930), contained one of the earliest depictions of computers in science fiction.

Through the early 1930s Campbell wrote stories of outer space but also began writing a different kind of science fiction under the pseudonym of "Don A. Stuart" (derived from his wife's name, Dona Stuart). In these stories, technology was secondary to the development of characterization and mood. One such story is "Twilight" (1934), in which machines work on incessantly, long after humans are gone.

Campbell's influence on other science fiction writers continued when he turned his attention in 1937 to editing *Astounding Stories*, later titled *Astounding Science Fiction*, then *Analog*. The magazine's contributors, including Isaac Asimov and Robert A. Heinlein, dominated the field in the mid-twentieth century. It was partly because of Campbell's influence that science

fiction came to address major social issues. Campbell died in Mountainside, N.J., on July 11, 1971.

ORSON SCOTT CARD

(b. 1951–)

Orson Scott Card rose to fame in the mid-1980s when his novel *Ender's Game* (1985) and its sequel *Speaker for the Dead* (1986) each won both the Hugo and Nebula awards for best novel. He was the only author to win both coveted science fiction awards in consecutive years.

Born on Aug. 24, 1951, Card was a descendent of Brigham Young, the leader of the Latter-day Saints and an early settler in the western United States. He majored in theater at Brigham Young University in Provo, Utah, and later founded the short-lived Utah Valley Repertory Theater Company. After financial troubles forced him to close the theater, Card took an editorial position with *Ensign*, the official magazine of the Latter-day Saints.

Card made his science fiction debut with the novella *Ender's Game* (1977), published in *Analogue* magazine. The story, which was later expanded into a full novel, laid the foundation for his most successful collection of writing, the *Ender* series, consisting of several novels and short stories that take place in a future where the existence of human beings is threatened by a militant alien race.

Card also published a parallel series known as the *Shadow Saga* that began with *Ender's Shadow* (1999); the events in both *Ender's Shadow* and *Ender's Game* occur in the same timeframe, and the two books share characters and action. He later employed the help of author Aaron Johnston to pen a prequel trilogy to the entire series known as the *First Formic War*.

Card also earned critical acclaim for the *Tales of Alvin Maker* series. Starting with *Seventh Son* (1987), the series is an alternate-history take on the nineteenth-century American frontier in which many people are born with supernatural powers. Critics have noted that the story of the protagonist, Alvin Maker, bears a resemblance to the life of Joseph Smith (1805–1844), the founder of the LDS.

Card was known to be outspoken when it came to his personal beliefs, which, at times, could alienate some audiences when it shone through in his writing. The two-book series composed of *Empire* (2006) and *Hidden Empire* (2009) was shunned by many readers and critics because of its preoccupation with divisive matters such as homosexuality.

ARTHUR C. CLARKE

(b. 1917–d. 2008)

The release in 1968 of the movie *2001: A Space Odyssey* gave international fame to Arthur C. Clarke, a science fiction writer whose reputation was already well established. His interest in science, however, went beyond fiction: his theories about satellite communications were borne out when the National Aeronautics and Space Administration (NASA) launched the Early Bird synchronous satellite in 1965.

Clarke was born on Dec. 16, 1917, at Minehead in Somerset, Eng. His interest in science developed in early childhood, and his fascination with science fiction began

Science fiction author Arthur C. Clarke, sitting in his Sri Lankan office in 2003. Luis Enrique Ascui/ Getty Images

in about 1930. Lacking money for college, Clarke worked in a government office in a job that left leisure to pursue his interest in space science. During World War II, as a radar instructor for the Royal Air Force, he published his first science fiction stories. In 1945 he wrote an article, "Extra-Terrestrial Relays," describing a satellite system that

would relay radio and television signals around the world. Released from the air force in 1946, Clarke enrolled in King's College, University of London. He received a bachelor of science degree in physics and mathematics in 1948.

Among the better-known of his science fiction works were *Childhood's End*, published in 1953, *A Fall of Moondust* (1961), *The Fountains of Paradise* (1979), and the short story "The Sentinel" (1951), on which *2001: A Space Odyssey* was based. Clarke and the movie's director, Stanley Kubrick, developed the short story into a novel (1968), published under the same name as the film. A sequel novel, *2010: Odyssey Two* (1982), by Clarke alone, was released as a film in 1984, and in 1997 he published *3001: The Final Odyssey*.

During the 1950s Clarke developed an interest in undersea exploration. From a home base in Ceylon (now Sri Lanka), he embarked on a career of skin diving and underwater photography, later described in a series of books beginning with *The Coast of Coral* (1956). He also wrote several nonfiction books on space. Clarke was knighted in 2000. He died on March 19, 2008, in Colombo, Sri Lanka.

SUSAN COOPER

(b. 1935–)

Although perhaps best known for her fantasy books for young adults, British-born U.S. author Susan Cooper also composed picture books for small children, adult fiction and nonfiction, newspaper pieces, and screenplays.

Susan Mary Cooper was born on May 23, 1935, in Burnham, Buckinghamshire, Eng. She attended Oxford University on a scholarship and had C.S. Lewis and J.R.R. Tolkien among her professors. Interested in journalism, she became the first female editor of Oxford's student newspaper, *Cherwell*, and landed a job with London's *Sunday Times* after graduation. When marriage to an American scientist brought her to Massachusetts in 1963, she helped ease her homesickness by writing columns about her new country for publication back in Britain.

Cooper entered the juvenile literature scene in 1965 with *Over Sea, Under Stone*, the first book in what became her popular *The Dark Is Rising* fantasy adventure series. The five-book sequence features ordinary and

supernatural characters involved in an epic struggle between the forces of good and evil. British and Welsh mythology and King Arthur legends figure prominently throughout. The second novel, *The Dark Is Rising* (1973), was chosen as a 1974 Newbery Honor Book and won the *Boston Globe–Horn Book* Award. After "Greenwitch" (1974), Cooper penned the Newbery Medal-winner *The Grey King* (1975). The series concluded with *Silver on the Tree* (1977), which the Welsh Arts Council honored with the Tir na N'og Award.

Cooper's other fantasy novels included *Seaward* (1983), *The Boggart* (1993), and *The Boggart and the Monster* (1997). For *Dawn of Fear* (1970), Cooper drew upon her memories of growing up in England during World War II. She also wrote the text for several picture books, including *Jethro and the Jumbie* (1979), *The Silver Cow: A Welsh Tale* (1983), *The Selkie Girl* (1986), and *Matthew's Dragon* (1991). Her adult works included the science fiction novel *Mandrake* (1964), the nonfiction book *Behind the Golden Curtain: A View of the U.S.A.* (1965), and the biography *J.B. Priestley: Portrait of an Author* (1970). Many of the speeches she gave during her career were collected in *Dreams and Wishes: Essays on Writing for Children* (1996).

Cooper collaborated with actor Hume Cronyn to write the stage play *Foxfire*, which ran in Canada and the United States during the early 1980s and was adapted for television in 1987. Cooper's other television writing credits included the films *The Dollmaker* (1984), *A Promise to Keep* (1990), and *To Dance with the White Dog* (1993). Several of her scripts were honored by the Writers Guild of America and earned Emmy nominations.

Cooper, divorced since 1982, and Cronyn, widowed in 1994 by the death of actress Jessica Tandy, married in July 1996. They were married until his death in 2003.

SAMUEL R. DELANY

(b. 1942–)

Writer and critic Samuel R. Delany published highly imaginative science fiction novels that address sexual, racial, and social issues; heroic quests; and the nature of language.

Born on April 1, 1942, in New York City, Samuel Ray Delany, Jr. attended City College of New York (now City University

of New York) in the early 1960s. His first
novel, *The Jewels of Aptor*, was published
in 1962, followed by *Babel-17* (1966), the
story of an artist-outsider that explores the
nature of language. Delany won the science
fiction Nebula Award for this book, which
established his reputation, and for *The
Einstein Intersection* (1967).

The issues of sexual identity and cul-
tural development were fully developed
in Delany's later works. *Dhalgren* (1975) is
the story of a young bisexual man search-
ing for identity in a large decaying city. In
Triton (1976), in which the main character
undergoes a sex-change operation, Delany
examines bias against women and homosexuals. Delany's *Nevèrÿon* series (*Tales of
Nevèrÿon* [1979]; *Neveryóna: Or, The Tale of
Signs and Cities* [1983]; *Flight from Nevèrÿon*
[1985]; and *The Bridge of Lost Desire* [1987])
is set in a magical past at the beginning of
civilization. These tales concern power and
its abuse while taking up contemporary
themes (including HIV/AIDS). His complex *Stars in My Pocket Like Grains of Sand*
(1984) was regarded by critics as a stylistic
breakthrough.

Delany also wrote the novella *Time
Considered as a Helix of Semi-precious Stones*

(1969) and the autobiographical *Atlantis: Three Tales* (1995), a collection of novellas recounting the experiences of young African American artists. Other autobiographical books include *The Motion of Light in Water: Sex and Science Fiction Writing in the East Village, 1957–1965* (1988), about his childhood and the beginning of his writing career, and *Bread & Wine: An Erotic Tale of New York* (1999), a memoir in graphic-novel format about his relationship with a white homeless man.

In 2000 Delany published *1984: Selected Letters*, a collection of correspondence with a friend. His subsequent novels include *Dark Reflections* (2007), which portrays the lackluster life of an aging gay African American poet. Delany's works on writing include *The Jewel-Hinged Jaw: Notes on the Language of Science Fiction* (1977), a groundbreaking critical analysis of science fiction.

PHILIP K. DICK

(b. 1928–d. 1982)

The novels and short stories of Philip K. Dick often depict the

psychological struggles of characters trapped in illusory environments. He was a prolific writer, sometimes completing a new work, usually a short story or a novella, every two weeks for printing in pulp paperback collections.

Philip Kindred Dick was born in Chicago, Ill., on Dec. 16, 1928. As a young man he worked briefly in radio before studying at the University of California, Berkeley, for one year. The publication of his first story, "Beyond Lies the Wub," in 1952 launched his full-time writing career. He published his first novel, *Solar Lottery*, in 1955.

Early in Dick's work the theme emerged that would remain his central preoccupation—that of a reality at odds with what it appeared or was intended to be. In such novels as *Time out of Joint* (1959), *The Man in the High Castle* (1962; Hugo Award winner), and *The Three Stigmata of Palmer Eldritch* (1965), the protagonists must determine their own place in an "alternate world." This theme continues in *The Simulacra* (1964) and culminates in *Do Androids Dream of Electric Sheep?* (1968), the latter of which was adapted for film as *Blade Runner* (1982).

Among Dick's numerous story collections are *A Handful of Darkness* (1955), *The Variable Man and Other Stories* (1957), *The Preserving Machine* (1969), and the posthumously published *I Hope I Shall Arrive Soon* (1985). In addition to *Electric Sheep*, several

A Russian journalist interviews a robotic version of science fiction author Philip K. Dick at the 2005 NextFest in Chicago, Ill. Much of Dick's work centered around androids and artificial intelligence. Scott Olson/ Getty Images

other of his works have been adapted for film: *We Can Remember It for You Wholesale* (filmed as *Total Recall* [1990 and 2012]), *Second Variety* (filmed as *Screamers* [1995]), *The Minority Report* (filmed as *Minority Report* [2002]), and *A Scanner Darkly* (1977; film 2006).

After years of drug abuse and mental illness, Dick died on March 2, 1982, in Santa Ana, Calif. At the time of his death, he was impoverished and had little literary reputation outside of science fiction circles. By the twenty-first century, however, he was widely regarded as a master of imaginative, paranoid fiction.

THOMAS MICHAEL DISCH

(b. 1940–d. 2008)

Thomas Michael Disch authored poetry, criticism, opera librettos, and plays that contained scathing social commentary and dark humor. These characteristics were readily apparent in works that were branded "New Wave" science fiction,

which he preferred to call "speculative" fiction.

Disch was born on Feb. 2, 1940, in Des Moines, Iowa. After his first short story was published in 1962, Disch dropped out of New York University's architecture program to become a writer. He produced his first novel, *The Genocides*, in 1965. His best-known science fiction novels—*Camp Concentration* (1968), *334* (1972), and *On Wings of Song* (1979)—are distinguished by their dark themes and biting satire. In *The Dreams Our Stuff Is Made Of: How Science Fiction Conquered the World* (1998), however, he criticized the genre, angering many science fiction fans but earning a Hugo Award (1999) in the process.

Many of his later works reflect his rejection of his Roman Catholic upbringing, notably the Gothic novel *The Priest* (1994) and the irreverent *The Word of God: Or, Holy Writ Rewritten* (2008). He also wrote sophisticated children's stories, notably "The Brave Little Toaster: A Bedtime Story for Small Appliances" (1986), which was adapted into an animated film in 1987. Disch died by his own hand on the Fourth of July in 2008.

HARLAN ELLISON

(b. 1934–)

Author Harlan Ellison is best known for his science fiction writing. Some of his more than one thousand short stories are considered classics of the genre. Nevertheless, Ellison wrote in a number of styles and rejected the label of science fiction writer as too limiting. In addition to short stories, he wrote novels, essays, and television and film scripts. His works are characterized by their humanistic themes and social commentary.

Harlan Jay Ellison was born on May 27, 1934, in Cleveland, Ohio. He briefly attended Ohio State University and later became a prolific contributor of science fiction, crime fiction, and true confessions to genre magazines. After serving in the United States Army (1957–59), he edited *Rogue* magazine from 1959 to 1960 and founded the publishing house Regency Books in 1960. Soon he became a successful television scriptwriter.

Ellison made his reputation as a science fiction writer with such short

Harlan Ellison (far right) *meeting with other television and film writers to discuss censorship, 1972.*
© AP Images

stories as "'Repent, Harlequin!' Said the Ticktockman" (1965), "A Boy and His Dog" (1969), and those in the collections *I Have No Mouth and I Must Scream* (1967) and *The Beast That Shouted Love at the Heart of the World* (1969). As an editor he published several important anthologies, including *Dangerous Visions* (1967) and *Again, Dangerous*

Visions (1972). Among Ellison's own collections are *Deathbird Stories: A Pantheon of Modern Gods* (1975), *All the Lies That Are My Life* (1980), *The Harlan Ellison Hornbook* (1990), *Mefisto in Onyx* (1993), and *Slippage: Precariously Poised, Previously Uncollected Stories* (1997). He won several Hugo and Nebula awards for his work.

Ellison also wrote several books of television and movie criticism and numerous screenplays, television series, and teleplays for series such as *Star Trek*, *Twilight Zone*, and *Babylon 5*.

PHILIP JOSÉ FARMER

(b. 1918–d. 2009)

Philip José Farmer combined fast-paced action with religious and political exploration in dozens of popular works. In addition to novels and novellas, he also wrote biographies of fictional characters, notably Tarzan and Doc Savage.

Born in Terra Haute, Ind., on Jan. 26, 1918, Farmer grew up in Peoria, Ill.

Allegedly his interest in science fiction occurred when he saw a zeppelin cruising through the skies of Peoria when he was six years old. He attended both the University of Missouri (1936) and Bradley University in Peoria (1941), eventually earning a degree in Greek from Bradley in 1950 after interruptions in his studies to get married and join the United States Army Air Corps.

Farmer worked in a Peoria steel mill and as a technical writer for General Electric Corp in Syracuse before bursting onto the literary scene in 1952 with the short story "The Lovers." The story—a shockingly frank exploration of sex between a human man and an insectoid alien female—won him a Hugo Award for best new writer in 1953. In the course of his career he was the recipient of two other Hugos, for his science fiction novella *Riders of the Purple Wage* (1968) and the novel *To Your Scattered Bodies Go* (the first *Riverworld* book; 1971).

Farmer was best known for his series of novels, including the *Riverworld, World of Tiers,* and *Dayworld* sequences. He also wrote *Venus on a Half Shell* (1974), which was published under the pseudonym Kilgore Trout—a fiction author created by writer Kurt Vonnegut.

Farmer was honored as a Nebula Award Grand Master by the Science Fiction and Fantasy Writers of America in 2001 and with the World Fantasy Award for Lifetime Achievement in 2001. Farmer died on February 25, 2009, in Peoria.

RAYMOND E. FEIST

(b. 1945–)

A nominee of five Locus Awards for best fantasy novel, Raymond E. Feist has been a leading writer within the genre for decades. Literary fame came to Feist almost overnight with the publication of his first novel *Magician* (1982), an epic fantasy that established him as a best-selling and internationally recognized author.

Born in 1945, in Southern California, Feist's birth name was Raymond Elias Gonzales III; at the age of nine, he decided to take the surname of his adoptive stepfather, Felix E. Feist. Growing up, he was influenced by historical and adventure fiction, which included the works of classical authors such as Robert

Fantasy author Raymond E. Feist. SFX Magazine/ Future/Getty Images

Louis Stevenson, Alexandre Dumas, and Thomas B. Costain.

While earning his bachelor's degree in communication arts from the University of California, San Diego, Feist became involved with a group of students who took part in fantasy role-playing. This activity allowed Feist to explore the creative process of developing

fantastical yet believable characters, story-lines, and worlds.

Feist primarily wrote novels and short stories that he considered to be "historical novels about another world." These works include *Magician* (1982), in the *Riftwar* series, and *Servant of the Empire* (1989), which was cowritten with Janny Wurts as the second novel of the *Empire Trilogy*. The latter won the Homer Award for fantasy novel.

The popularity of Feist's imaginative lands led to the creation of the role-playing computer games *Betrayal at Krondor* (1993) and *Return to Krondor* (1998). Feist continued writing installments of the *Riftwar Cycle* well into the twenty-first century, including *A Crown Imperilled* (2012) and a final book in the series, appropriately titled *Magician's End* (2013).

NEIL GAIMAN

(b. 1960–)

K nown for his witty, often dark sense of humor and imagination, British

writer Neil Gaiman has published numerous works. Along with children's books, graphic novels, and comics, he has won acclaim as the author of science fiction and fantasy novels.

Neil Richard Gaiman was born on Nov. 10, 1960, in Portchester, Hampshire, Eng. He graduated from the Whitgift School in Croydon. Gaiman turned to journalism after his first attempts to become published led to a string of rejections. He established his credibility as a writer after publishing a biography of the English band Duran Duran in 1984. Shortly thereafter, Gaiman worked with artist Dave McKean on the graphic novel *Violent Cases* (1987). He went on to win audiences with his dark humor in *Black Orchid* (1988) and again in *Sandman* (1989–96), which won a World Fantasy Award for short fiction.

At the same time, Gaiman ventured into the world of adult novels. His notoriety from collaborating with Douglas Adams and the subsequent book *Don't Panic: The Official Hitchhiker's Guide to the Galaxy Companion* (1988) caught the attention of such established novelists as Terry Pratchett. In 1990 Gaiman and Pratchett coauthored the novel *Good Omens*. Gaiman

British author Neil Gaiman, who is noteworthy as a darkly humorous children's and young adult writer as well as a science fiction and fantasy novelist. © Philippe Matsas—HarperCollins Children's Books

then wrote *Neverwhere* (1996), which was based on the popular BBC television series that he also wrote and produced. He also published *Stardust* (1999), a book that was turned into a film in 2007.

Gaiman's *American Gods* (2001) won the Hugo Award in 2002 for outstanding novel as well as the Nebula Award for science fiction and fantasy, and Gaiman revisited some of the same characters in *Anansi Boys* (2005). In 2003–04 he penned eight issues of *1602* for Marvel Comics.

WILLIAM GIBSON

(b. 1948–)

The American-Canadian writer William Gibson was the leader of the science fiction genre's cyberpunk movement. Cyberpunk combines a cynical, tough "punk" sensibility with futuristic cybernetic (i.e., having to do with mechanical-electrical communication) technology.

William Ford Gibson was born in Conway, S.C., on March 17, 1948, and

grew up in southwestern Virginia. After dropping out of high school in 1967, he traveled to Canada and eventually settled there, earning a B.A. (1977) from the University of British Columbia.

Many of Gibson's early stories, including "Johnny Mnemonic" (1981; film 1995) and "Burning Chrome" (1982), were published in *Omni* magazine. His first novel, *Neuromancer* (1984), won three major science fiction awards (the Nebula, the Hugo, and the Philip K. Dick awards) and established Gibson's reputation as a sci-fi writer. The novel also helped him emerge as a leading exponent of cyberpunk, a new school of science fiction writing. Gibson's creation of "cyberspace," a computer-simulated reality that foreshadowed virtual reality technology, is considered the author's major contribution to the science fiction genre.

Count Zero (1986) was set in the same world as *Neuromancer* but seven years later. Gibson followed that novel with *Mona Lisa Overdrive* (1988). After collaborating with writer Bruce Sterling on *The Difference Engine* (1990), a story set in Victorian England, Gibson returned

"Cyberpunk" author William Gibson, attending a literature festival in Rome in 2007. Ron Bull/Toronto Star/Getty Images

to the subject of cyberspace in *Virtual Light* (1993). His *Idoru* (1996), set in twenty-first-century Tokyo, focuses on the media and virtual celebrities of the future. Gibson's other works include *All Tomorrow's Parties* (1999) and a trilogy of books: *Pattern Recognition* (2003), *Spook*

Country (2007), and *Zero History* (2010). In 2012 Gibson published a collection of nonfiction, *Distrust That Particular Flavor.*

JOE HALDEMAN

(b. 1943–)

A 2012 inductee into the Science Fiction Hall of Fame, Joe Haldeman is best known for writings inspired by his experience as a soldier during the Vietnam War, as well as his adjustment to civilian life upon returning home.

Joseph William Haldeman was born in Oklahoma City, Okla., on June 9, 1943. He spent much of youth growing up in different locations, including Puerto Rico; New Orleans, La.; Washington, D.C.; and Anchorage, Alaska. His older brother was science fiction author Jack C. Haldeman II (1941–2002).

After graduating from the University of Maryland with a bachelor's degree in physics and astronomy in 1967, Joe Haldeman was drafted into the Vietnam War as a combat engineer (1968–69). While on duty,

he suffered serious injuries and was awarded
the Purple Heart. After returning home
from war, Haldeman wrote the short story
"Out of Phase" (1969), which was published in *Galaxy* magazine. His first novel,
War Year (1972), was a traditional fiction
piece that could be described as a semi-
autobiographical story, detailing a combat

*Joe Haldeman gives attendees of Spain's 2010 Dark
Week event in Gijon a glimpse of a work in progress.*
Juan Carlos Rojas/Notimex/Newscom

engineer's experience during the Vietnam War and the camaraderie established within his platoon.

Haldeman's first critical success came with *The Forever War* (1975). The novel follows soldiers that leap into the future to fight wars against an alien species on distant planets. Lacking a way to travel back to their own time, they face alienation from the people of the future for whom they were sent to fight. Many critics see the book as an allegory of the experience of Vietnam soldiers when they returned to America. The book earned Haldeman both the Hugo and Nebula awards in 1976. More than two decades later, he published the follow-up novels *Forever Peace* (1997), which also won the Hugo and Nebula awards, and *Forever Free* (1999).

One of the few works that Haldeman became known for that didn't employ a military element was the novella *The Hemingway Hoax* (1990), which was published in *Isaac Asimov's Science Fiction* magazine. The piece, which earned Haldeman another set of Hugo and Nebula awards, was later published as a full-length novel. In 2010, Haldeman was honored by the Science Fiction Writers of America's guild with the prestigious

Grand Master Award for his contributions to the genre.

HARRY HARRISON

(b. 1925–d. 2012)

Henry Harrison was the author of more than sixty books but was best known for his novel *Make Room! Make Room!* (1966), a chilling look at a futuristic society competing for scarce resources. The book was adapted into the classic science fiction film *Soylent Green* in 1973.

Born Henry Maxwell Dempsey on March 12, 1925, Harrison initially worked as an illustrator for pulp magazines. He branched into writing in the 1950s. He helmed the *Flash Gordon* comic strip throughout the 1950s and '60s.

Harrison often tweaked convention with satiric takes on science fiction clichés. According to the *New York Times*, his 1965 novel *Bill the Galactic Hero* was a satiric response to science fiction author Robert A. Heinlein's *Starship Troopers*. Harrison's most enduring character, the time-jumping con man James Bolivar diGriz (better known as the Stainless Steel Rat), appeared in a dozen books, concluding with *The Stainless Steel Rat Returns* (2010).

Harrison has been credited with writing some 100 short stories and a science fiction textbook; he also toiled as the editor of numerous anthologies and a science fiction literary journal. In 2004 he was inducted into the Science Fiction and Fantasy Hall of Fame. Harrison died in Brighton, East Sussex, Eng., on Aug. 15, 2012.

ROBERT A. HEINLEIN

(b. 1907–d. 1988)

The American author Robert A. Heinlein helped raise the level of science fiction to a respected form of literary expression. His writing reflected his training in science and technology along with an interest in language, economics, history, and sociology. He won an unprecedented four Hugo science fiction awards.

Robert Anson Heinlein was born on July 7, 1907, in Butler, Mo. After graduating from the United States Naval Academy in 1929, he served as an officer in the navy for five years. He spent some time at the University of California at Los Angeles studying mathematics and physics. His first magazine story was published in 1939 and his first novel, *Rocket Ship Galileo*, in 1947. The novel was the basis for his screenplay for the motion picture *Destination Moon* (1950). His fiction often anticipated scientific and technical advances, such as the atomic bomb and the waterbed. His most popular book was *Stranger in a Strange Land* (1961), which became a hippie handbook and introduced the verb grok (meaning "to know intuitively, totally").

Heinlein's books include *Beyond This Horizon* (1948), *Red Planet* (1949), *Sixth Column* (1949), *The Puppet Masters* (1951), *Revolt in 2100* (1953), *Starman Jones* (1953), *Tunnel in the Sky* (1955), *The Menace from Earth* (1959), *The Moon Is a Harsh Mistress* (1966), *The Number of the Beast* (1980), *Expanded Universe* (1980), and *Friday* (1982). *Green Hills of Earth* (1951) is a short-story collection. He died in Carmel, Calif., on May 8, 1988.

FRANK HERBERT

(b. 1920–d. 1986)

A merican science fiction writer Frank Herbert is noted as the author of the best-selling *Dune* series of futuristic novels. The books explore such themes as ecology, human evolution, and psychic possibilities.

Frank Patrick Herbert was born on Oct. 8, 1920, in Tacoma, Wash. Before he began to write full-time, in 1972, Herbert held a variety of jobs. He was working as a journalist when his reputation was made with the publication of *Dune* (1965; filmed by David Lynch in 1984), which was translated into fourteen languages and sold some twelve million copies. *Dune* had been rejected by 20 publishers before it was published. Its sequels are *Dune Messiah* (1969), *Children of Dune* (1976), *God-Emperor of Dune* (1981), *Heretics of Dune* (1984), and *Chapterhouse: Dune* (1985). In the late 1990s Herbert's son Brian began collaborating with Kevin J. Anderson on a series of prequels to the *Dune* chronicles; *Dune: House Atreides* was released in 1999.

Included among Herbert's more than two dozen novels are the highly acclaimed

Portrait of Dune *writer Frank Herbert, 1978.* Ulf Andersen/Getty Images

Dragon in the Sea (1956), *The Green Brain* (1966), *The Santaroga Barrier* (1968), *The Heaven Makers* (1968), *The God Makers* (1972), and *The Dosadi Experiment* (1977). Herbert died on Feb. 11, 1986, in Madison, Wis.

ROBERT E. HOWARD

(b. 1906–d. 1936)

U.S. author Robert E. Howard had a short-lived career, yet he had a long-lasting impact upon the fantasy genre. His short stories, numbering more than 300, were revered by peers and fans alike—especially for their larger-than-life, heroic characters.

Born in Peaster, Texas, on January 22, 1906, Robert Ervin Howard was raised in several rural towns throughout the state. An avid reader from an early age—he claimed to have "raided school houses" in search of books—he was inspired by the adventure stories of Sir Arthur Conan Doyle, Mark Twain, and Rudyard Kipling, as well as the fantasy and horror writings of H.P. Lovecraft.

Throughout his twelve-year career, Howard produced short stories in a broad range of genres, including sports, science fiction, western, mystery, horror, and fantasy. His first published piece was "Spear and Fang" (1925), which was featured in *Weird Tales* magazine when he was just eighteen. His most notable works centered around the adventures of heroes such as the character Kull of Atlantis, whose first appearance in the story "The Shadow Kingdom" established a new subgenre of fantasy known as "sword and sorcery."

Howard's most famous character, though, was Conan the Barbarian, first introduced to readers in the short story "The Phoenix on the Sword" (1932), also featured in *Weird Tales*. Conan quickly became a fan favorite. Howard published seventeen more stories with this popular protagonist between 1932 and 1936; four more were posthumous releases. The Conan series has frequently been anthologized since Howard's death, more recently with the collection *The Complete Chronicles of Conan: Centenary Edition* (2007).

For reasons that are unclear, Howard committed suicide on June 11, 1936, at the age of thirty. Though his career was cut short, his legacy lived on well into the twenty-first century in the form of comic books, cartoon series, and feature-length films that were based on his fan-beloved character Conan.

DAMON FRANCIS KNIGHT

(b. 1922–d. 2002)

Damon Francis Knight wrote more than a dozen science fiction novels and more than 100 short stories within the genre. The best known of these is "To Serve Man" (1950), which was adapted for the television series *The Twilight Zone* and became a classic. Knight made an even greater impact on the genre as an editor and critic.

Knight was born in Baker City, Ore., on September 19, 1922. In the 1940s, as a member of the Futurians, a group of influential writers, he began his mission of raising the standards of science fiction writing and treating it as serious literature. Knight founded in 1956 with James Blish and Judith

Merril the Milford Science Fiction Writers' Conference and in 1965 the Science Fiction Writers of America. He also edited dozens of anthologies.

In 1994, Knight was given the Nebula Grand Master Award in recognition of his many achievements. He died in Eugene, Ore., on April 15, 2002.

C.M. KORNBLUTH

(b. 1923–d. 1958)

The stories of American science fiction writer C.M. Kornbluth reflect a dark view of the future. He was a member of the Futurians, a group of young science fiction fans that included members who went on to become some of the most influential authors and editors in the genre.

Born in New York City in 1923, Kornbluth published science fiction stories as a teenager. After army service during World War II, he attended the University of Chicago. Along with other Futurians Isaac Asimov and Frederik Pohl, Kornbluth composed and edited most of the tales in such sci-fi magazines as *Astonishing Stories*

and *Super Science Stories*. Extremely prolific, Kornbluth wrote under almost twenty
pseudonyms, including S.D. Gottesman,
Cecil Corwin, Simon Eisner, Jordan Park,
and Cyril Judd (a joint pseudonym with
author Judith Merril).

Critics praised Kornbluth's well-plotted
fiction for its vision and emphasis on social
concerns. Critical of stories in which science was presented as the ultimate savior
of humanity, he instead examined the dangers of technology allowed to run amok.
Much of his work was serialized in *Galaxy
Science Fiction*. Kornbluth also wrote *Takeoff*
(1952), a science fiction detective novel
about the first space flight, and *The Syndic*
(1953), about organized crime in a futuristic
United States.

Kornbluth also wrote in collaboration
with other science fiction authors. With
Merril he wrote such works as *Outpost
Mars* (1952; revised as *Sin in Space*, 1961)
and *Gunner Cade* (1952). Among the books
he published with Pohl are *Search the Sky*
(1954), a satire on space colonization, and
Gladiator-at-Law (1955).

Kornbluth died of a heart attack at age
thirty-five on March 21, 1958, in Waverly,
N.Y. His essay "The Failure of the Science

Fiction Novel as Social Criticism" was published posthumously in 1959.

NANCY KRESS

(b. 1948–)

Following a successful transition from writing primarily fantasy, Nancy Kress established herself as a master of science fiction short stories and novels. Many of these works centered on social and genetic engineering.

Kress was born in Buffalo, N.Y., on Jan. 20, 1948, and earned a degree in elementary education from State University of New York at Plattsburgh. After a short stint teaching, she became a stay-at-home mother and began writing in her free time. Her first short story was the science fiction piece "The Earth Dwellers" (1976), which appeared in *Galaxy* magazine. Her first full-length works were grounded in fantasy, including *The Prince of Morning Bells* (1981), *The Golden Grove* (1984), and *The White Pipes* (1985).

Kress first found critical recognition with the release of *Trinity and Other Stories* (1985), a collection of short stories that includes "Out of All Them Bright Stories," which won the Nebula Award (short form).

Following the short-story collection's success, Kress directed her writing toward science fiction. Her first published novel in the genre was *An Alien Light* (1988), followed by *Brain Rose* (1990). Her most popular work within the genre was the Hugo and Nebula award-winning novella *Beggars in Spain* (1991; full-length novel, 1993). Kress also wrote the sequels *Beggars & Choosers* (1994) and *Beggars Ride* (1996).

Kress found further success with the novellas *The Flowers of Aulit Prison* (1996), *Fountain of Age* (2007), and *The Erdmann Nexus* (2008). Her short fiction has been published in several collections, including *Future Perfect: Six Stories of Genetic Engineering* (2012), *The Body Human: Three Stories of Future Medicine* (2012), and *Fountain of Age: Stories* (2012).

URSULA K. LE GUIN

(b. 1929–)

Ursula K. Le Guin wrote science fiction and fantasy stories for children. She

is best known, however, for the works she wrote for adult readers, which frequently feature highly detailed descriptions of alien societies. In 2000, she was awarded the Living Legend medal by the Library of Congress.

The daughter an anthropologist and a writer, Le Guin was born on Oct. 21, 1929, in Berkeley, Calif. She attended Radcliffe College (B.A., 1951) and Columbia University (M.A., 1952). Her first three novels, *Rocannon's World* (1966), *Planet of Exile* (1966), and *City of Illusions* (1967), revolve around alien beings who establish life on other planets, including Earth. Among Le Guin's most significant novels were *The Left Hand of Darkness* (1969), *The Dispossessed* (1974), *The Word for World Is Forest* (1972), and *Always Coming Home* (1985). In 2008 Le Guin made literary news with *Lavinia*, a tale told from the point of view of a minor character from Virgil's *Aeneid*, describing in full her role in the historical development of early Rome.

Le Guin also created a series of books—*A Wizard of Earthsea* (1968), *The Tombs of Atuan* (1971), *The Farthest Shore* (1972), *Tehanu* (1990), *Tales from Earthsea* (2001), and *The Other Wind* (2001)—for

Science fiction and fantasy writer Ursula K. Le Guin, after receiving a literary award for children's literature in 2005. Amy Graves/WireImage/Getty Images

children. The *Earthsea* series gained a considerable number of adult readers as well. She tapped the young adult market again with her *Annals of the Western Shore* series, which includes *Gifts* (2004), *Voices* (2006), and *Powers* (2007). Le Guin also wrote a series about cats with wings titled, appropriately, the *Catwings Tales*.

The essay collections *The Language of the Night* (1979), *Dancing at the Edge of the World* (1989), *Steering the Craft* (1998), and *The Wave in the Mind* (2004) offer glimpses of Le Guin's take on fantasy fiction, feminist issues, writing, and other topics. Her volumes of poetry include *Wild Angels* (1975), *Wild Oats and Fireweed* (1988), *Going Out with Peacocks and Other Poems* (1994), *Incredible Good Fortune* (2006), and *Finding My Elegy: New and Selected Poems 1960–2010* (2012).

FRITZ LEIBER

(b. 1910–d. 1992)

Fritz Leiber was noted for his literary innovation. His works focus on the sword-and-sorcery, contemporary horror, and satiric science fiction subgenres.

Born in Chicago, Ill., on Dec. 24, 1910, Fritz Reuter Leiber, Jr. was the son of stage and film actors. Leiber performed onstage and in films himself before his first published story, "Two Sought Adventure," appeared in 1939. The characters in that story were featured in a series of swashbuckling adventure fantasies collected in *The Three of Swords* (1989) and *Swords' Masters* (1990).

Leiber was also a pioneer of horror stories with modern urban settings. These include the short story "Smoke Ghost" (1941) and continue in his early novels such as *Gather, Darkness!* (1950) and *Conjure Wife* (1953).

Leiber's fiction in the early 1950s, including the short story "Coming Attraction" (1950) and the novel *The Green Millennium* (1953), was noted for its satire of what he saw as the decay of American society. The satire is less harsh in his later fiction, which includes *The Silver Eggheads* (1961) and *A Specter Is Haunting Texas* (1969). His later short stories, such as "Gonna Roll the Bones" (1967), "Ill Met in Lankhmar" (1970), and "Belsen Express" (1975), are among his most admired works.

Leiber died on Sept. 5, 1992, in San Francisco, Calif. His supernatural novella

The Dealings of Daniel Kesserich—among the first science fiction and fantasy stories he ever wrote (1936)—was published posthumously in 1997.

STANISŁAW LEM

(b. 1921–d. 2006)

The work of Polish science fiction author Stanisław Lem veers between humanism and despair about human limitations. His books have been translated into more than thirty-five languages.

Lem was born in Lwów, Poland (now Lviv, Ukraine) on Sept. 12, 1921. The son of a doctor, Lem studied medicine at Lvov Medical Institute (now Lviv State Medical University) during 1940–41, but his education was interrupted by the German occupation of Poland during World War II. After the Soviet Union recaptured the city in 1944, he resumed his studies. Although he eventually received a certificate of completion of medical studies, he did not take the final medical exams.

Beginning in 1946, Lem's first novel, *Człowiek z Marsa* ("The Man from Mars"), was serialized in the Polish magazine *Nowy Świat Przygód* ("New World of Adventures"). While working as a scientific research assistant between 1947 and 1950, Lem also published poems, short stories, and scientific essays. An early work—*Szpital Przemienienia* (1955; *Hospital of the Transfiguration*)—written in 1948 as a full-length novel, was initially suppressed by Communist Party censors. Two years later Lem wrote first work of science fiction, *Astronauci* (1951; "The Astronauts"). Publication of the book, which was later adapted for an East German film, convinced him to become a full-time writer.

Lem blossomed as a serious international science fiction author, writing some seventeen books in the next dozen years. Lem's renown rests primarily on three works: *Solaris* (1961; adapted for film in 1972 and 2002), *Głos Pana* (1968; *His Master's Voice*), and *Cyberiada* (1965; subtitled *Fables for the Cybernetic Age*).

Although certain themes recur in all his works, his fiction can be divided into two major groups. The first includes his traditional science fiction, with its vividly imagined fantasies of technological advances, space travel, and alien worlds, such as *Eden* (1959; Eng. trans. *Eden*), *Powrót z gwiazd* (1961; *Return from the Stars*),

Niezwyciężony (1964; *The Invincible*), and *Opowieści o pilocie Pirxie* (1968; *Tales of Pirx the Pilot*). The second group contains dark fables such as *Dzienniki gwiazdowe* (1957; *The Star Diaries*) and *Pamiętnik znaleziony w wannie* (1961; *Memoirs Found in a Bathtub*).

In addition to his fiction, Lem also wrote *Summa technologiae* (1964), a survey of prospective social and scientific advances, and criticism of the science fiction genre in volumes such as *Fantastyka i futurologia* (1970), portions of which were translated with other material in *Microworlds* (1984). His scathing evaluations of other sci-fi writers' work led the Science Fiction Writers of America, which had granted him an honorary membership in 1973, to oust him in 1976. Lem died in Kraków, Poland on March 27, 2006.

MADELEINE L'ENGLE

(b. 1918–d. 2007)

American author Madeleine L'Engle came into prominence with her 1962 children's novel *A Wrinkle in Time*, which won the 1963 Newbery Medal. The novel is a science fiction story with philosophical and religious elements.

She was born Madeleine L'Engle Camp on Nov. 29, 1918, in New York City. She received a B.A. degree in 1941 from Smith College and later studied at Columbia University. She acted in the theater in the 1940s and taught at private grade schools in New York.

L'Engle's *A Wrinkle in Time* and many of her other books for young readers pit good against evil while interweaving elements of fantasy and philosophy. These included sequels to *A Wrinkle in Time*, such as *A Wind in the Door* (1973) and *A Swiftly Tilting Planet* (1978), as well as *Camilla Dickinson* (1951), *The Moon by Night* (1963), *The Young Unicorns* (1968), *Dragons in the Waters* (1976), and *A Ring of Endless Light* (1980).

L'Engle also wrote works for adults, including poems, articles, and stories for several magazines. Among her volumes of poetry were *Lines Scribbled on an Envelope* (1969) and *The Weather of the Heart* (1978). She also published a series of autobiographical works based on her journals, including *The Summer of the Great-Grandmother* (1974) and *The Irrational Season* (1977).

In 1980 L'Engle won the American Book Award for *A Swiftly Tilting Planet*, and in

1981 *A Ring of Endless Light* was named a Newbery Honor Book. L'Engle had a following of loyal readers who were drawn by her imaginative and wide-ranging tales that were filled with symbols and elaborate plot twists. She died on Sept. 6, 2007, in Litchfield, Conn.

C.S. LEWIS

(b. 1898–d. 1963)

C.S. Lewis was best known as an apologist for Christianity. Yet he also wrote a trilogy of religious science fiction novels, as well as a series of fantasy novels for children.

Clive Staples Lewis was born in Belfast, Ireland, on Nov. 29, 1898. He was educated by private tutor and then at Malvern College in England for a year before attending University College, Oxford, in 1916. His education was interrupted by service in World War I. In 1918 he returned to Oxford, where he did outstanding work as a classical scholar. He taught at Magdalen College, Oxford, from

1925 to 1954, and from 1954 until his death in Oxford he was professor of medieval and Renaissance English at Cambridge University in Cambridge. He was highly respected in his field of study, both as a teacher and writer.

Lewis's science fiction series contains the novels *Out of the Silent Planet* (1938), *Perelandra* (1943), and *That Hideous Strength* (1945). The first novel in the trilogy is, in part, a retelling of the Christ story. It is an account of the voyage of Ransom, a linguist, to the planet Malacandra (Mars), where he learns that Thulcandra (Earth) is called the silent planet because there has been no communication from it in years. The novel gives voice to Lewis's concerns about the secularization of society and argues that a return to traditional religious belief is the only means of salvation.

Perlandra was also published as *Voyage to Venus: Perelandra*. It takes up the adventures of the hero Ransom, who struggles with an evil scientist over the fate of the planet Venus. In an obvious reference to the biblical story of the temptation of Eve, the novel presents the scientist as the tempter of the female ruler of Venus.

Though known mainly for his works on Christian thought and values, C.S. Lewis also wrote a science fiction trilogy and a series of fantasy books for children. Wolf Suschitzky/Time & Life Pictures/Getty Images

Although sometimes criticized for its sexist view of women, *Perelandra* nevertheless is successful as both science fiction and religious allegory.

For children Lewis wrote a series of seven allegorical fantasy tales known collectively as *The Chronicles of Narnia*. The seven books in the series are *The Lion, the Witch, and the Wardrobe* (1950), *Prince Caspian* (1951), *The Voyage of the "Dawn Treader"* (1952), *The Silver Chair* (1953), *The Horse and His Boy* (1954), *The Magician's Nephew* (1955), and *The Last Battle* (1956). Lewis wrote the works for his goddaughter Lucy Pevensie, who—with her siblings Susan, Edmund, and Peter—figures as a character in the series. The kingdom's first years are told in *The Magician's Nephew*. The series is considered a classic of fantasy literature.

The death of C.S. Lewis on Nov. 22, 1963, was not much noticed at the time because it occurred on the same day as the assassination of United States president John F. Kennedy. Yet for three decades Lewis had been one of the most widely read authors on Christian teaching in the Western world.

H.P. LOVECRAFT

(b. 1890–d. 1937)

Author H.P. Lovecraft was mostly known for his tales of horror and fantasy, which he did not start writing until a relatively late age. He made his living as a ghostwriter and rewrite man and spent most of his life in seclusion and poverty. His fame as a writer increased after his death.

Howard Phillips Lovecraft was born on Aug. 20, 1890, in Providence, R.I. He was interested in science from childhood, but lifelong poor health prevented him from attending college.

Lovecraft began his writing career as a journalist in 1915. By 1917 he started writing science fiction stories that over his twenty-year career were mostly published in the magazine *Weird Tales*. His *Cthulhu Mythos* series of tales describe ordinary New Englanders' encounters with horrific extraterrestrial beings. His other short stories deal with similarly terrifying phenomena. *The Case of Charles Dexter Ward* (1927; published in 1941), *At the Mountains*

of Madness and *The Shadow over Innsmouth* (both written in 1931 and published in 1936) are considered his best short novels.

Lovecraft was a master of poetic language, and he attained unusually high literary standards in the science fiction genre. He died in Providence on March 15, 1937.

GEORGE R.R. MARTIN

(b. 1948–)

F antasy author George R.R. Martin is best known for his *A Song of Ice and Fire* series (1996–), a bloody saga about various factions vying for control of a fictional kingdom. The books became the basis of a popular cable television series, *Game of Thrones.*

Born Sept. 20, 1948, in Bayonne, N.J., George Raymond Richard Martin attended Northwestern University and graduated with bachelor's (1970) and master's (1971) degrees in journalism. Having received conscientious objector status

during the Vietnam War, Martin fulfilled his alternative military service by volunteering for a legal assistance organization in Chicago, while earning his living as an organizer of chess tournaments and writing short fiction.

Martin had been an aficionado of science fiction and fantasy literature since childhood. As an adult, he frequently attended science fiction and fantasy conventions. Writing fantasy stories seemed like a natural fit.

Martin sold his first short story in 1971. Shortly thereafter, he won a Hugo Award (1974) for his sci-fi novella *A Song for Lya*. In 1977, a year after he had accepted a position teaching journalism at Clarke College in Iowa, Martin released his first work of full-length fiction, *Dying of the Light*. Two years later he moved to Santa Fe, New Mexico, to write full-time.

Martin received both the Hugo and the Nebula awards for his novelette *Sandkings* (1981). That year he also released *Windhaven* (cowritten with Lisa Tuttle), about a girl who gains the ability to fly, followed by two full-length efforts, the vampire novel *Fevre Dream* (1982) and the

rock-and-roll horror tale *The Armageddon Rag* (1983). Though the latter sold poorly, a producer optioned the film rights. The film was never made, but the producer suggested Martin as a writer for a remake of *The Twilight Zone* series in 1985. He wrote several screenplays for the show before accepting a position as a writer for the TV series *Beauty and the Beast* (1987–90); he eventually became a producer for the modernized fairy tale.

Martin returned to long-form fiction in 1991, having had no luck selling his television pilots and screenplays. One of his efforts evolved into *A Game of Thrones* (1996), the first in what was initially intended to be a trilogy set largely in the imagined Seven Kingdoms of the land of Westeros. The series favored a bleak realism. Major characters—even sympathetic ones—frequently met grisly ends, and the plots were dominated by the political intriguing and battlefield savagery of those questing for the titular throne. Further installments include *A Clash of Kings* (1999), *A Storm of Swords* (2000), *A Feast for Crows* (2005), and *A Dance with Dragons* (2011). The series was adapted

Fantasy author George R.R. Martin (center) *enthroned among cast members of the HBO television series* Game of Thrones, *based on his series of books by the same name.* Alberto E. Rodriguez/ Getty Images

as an HBO show that premiered in 2011. Martin served as an executive producer and contributed scripts for several episodes.

In the course of his career, Martin also edited numerous sci-fi and fantasy

anthologies. His short stories were compiled in *GRRM: A Retrospective* (2003).

ANNE MCCAFFREY

(b. 1926–d. 2011)

A merican-born Irish science fiction writer Anne McCaffrey vanquished chauvinistic science fiction and fantasy genre conceits with her depictions of fierce female protagonists. She was most noted for her *Dragonriders of Pern* series, which spanned more than twenty books.

Anne Inez McCaffrey was born April 1, 1926, in Cambridge, Mass. She graduated (1947) with a bachelor's degree in Slavonic languages and literature from Radcliffe College in Cambridge. Her first story was published in *Science Fiction + Magazine*. In 1967, she published her first novel, *Restoree*. According to her official biography, McCaffrey wrote the book as a way to challenge the stereotypical portrayals of women in science fiction novels that had come before.

In 1968 McCaffrey released *Dragonflight*, the first of her novels set on the mythical

planet of Pern, in which humans and dragons collaborate to combat fungal spores from outer space. Among the other novels by McCaffrey are the books of the *Crystal Singer, Freedom*, and *The Ship Who Sang* series.

McCaffrey moved to Ireland in 1970, having learned of an income-tax exemption offered to writers. She was the first woman to win the Hugo (1968) and Nebula (1969) awards, given for science fiction and fantasy writing, respectively. The last installment in the series, *Dragon's Time* (written with her son Todd), appeared in 2011. McCaffrey died Nov. 21, 2011, in Newcastle, County Wicklow, Ireland.

WALTER M. MILLER

(b. 1922–d. 1996)

U.S. science fiction writer Walter M. Miller wrote of the promise and the dangers of science and technology. His best-known work is his only full-length novel, *A Canticle for Leibowitz*.

Walter Michael Miller, Jr. was born on Jan. 23, 1922, in New Smyrna Beach, Fla. He briefly attended the University of Tennessee before joining the United States Army Air Corps as a pilot during World War II. After the war he returned to school at the University of Texas and studied engineering.

Miller began writing in 1950. His early work included numerous science fiction short stories as well as scripts for the television show *Captain Video.* Between 1955 and 1957 Miller published three novellas—*Fiat Homo, Fiat Lux,* and *Fiat Voluntas Tua*—that he eventually incorporated into one novel, *A Canticle for Leibowitz* (1960). The book, which centers on the events following a nuclear holocaust, won Miller considerable fame and a cult-like following. It was awarded the Hugo Award in 1961.

Miller did not publish any new work after the release of *A Canticle for Leibowitz.* Many of his short stories were republished, however, in *Conditionally Human* (1962) and *The View from the Stars* (1964), which were later combined in *The Short Stories of Walter M. Miller* (1978). Miller committed suicide in January 1996, soon after the unexpected death of his wife, Anne.

LARRY NIVEN

(b. 1938–)

A t the same time that Larry Niven's first published short story about the dark side of Mercury was published, scientists announced the discovery that the planet was not actually locked in its rotation and did, in fact, revolve around the Sun—nullifying the premise of the story. Nonetheless, Niven continued to write science fiction grounded in theoretical physics, becoming one of the genre's most prolific writers.

Laurence van Cott Niven was born on April 30, 1938. He began his writing career after dropping out of a graduate program for mathematics at the University of California, Los Angeles. His first piece to be published was the short story "The Coldest Place" (1964), which he sold for $25 to *If* magazine.

Many of Niven's works take place in a setting dubbed "Known Space." "Neutron Star" (1966), for example, is a short story that follows space pilot Beowulf Shaeffer as he attempts to discover the cause of destruction of a starship that was surveying a neutron star—a concept that, at the time, was merely hypothetical. "Neutron Star"earned Niven his first Hugo Award.

Niven's most well-received novel was the Hugo and Nebula award-winning *Ringworld* (1970). The book was followed by three sequels and four prequels, including the Hugo- and Nebula-nominated *The Ringworld Engineers* (1979).

Niven was widely acclaimed for his body of work and was recognized for his contributions to the science fiction genre with the Skylark Award in 1973 and the 2003 Robert A. Heinlein Award.

FREDERIK POHL

(b. 1919–)

S cience fiction writer Frederik Pohl uses the genre as a mode of social criticism. His best works explore the long-range consequences of technology in an ailing society.

A high school dropout, Pohl served in the U.S. Army Air Force during World War II. He worked briefly in an advertising agency before returning to writing and editing. He began his professional career in science fiction by editing some of the classic stories of

the genre, then collaborating with many of its best representatives. He edited two science fiction magazines, *Astonishing Stories* and *Super Science Stories.*

In the late 1930s Pohl and others interested in science fiction formed a group known as the Futurians, which dedicated itself to the creation and promotion of constructive and forward-looking ("futurian") science fiction. Other members included Isaac Asimov and C.M. Kornbluth.

Though many of his works are known for their humor, Pohl often addressed serious issues. His most famous work, *The Space Merchants* (1953), was written in collaboration with Kornbluth. This chilling portrait of a world dominated by the economic perspective of advertising executives made Pohl's reputation. Pohl wrote several other books with Kornbluth; some of their work can be found in *Our Best: The Best of Frederik Pohl and C.M. Kornbluth* (1987).

Pohl's other novels include *The Age of the Pussyfoot* (1969); the Nebula Award winner *Man Plus* (1976); *Gateway* (1977), which won both the Hugo and the Nebula awards for best novel; *Jem* (1980), which won the American Book Award; and *Chernobyl* (1987). The trilogy composed of *The Other End of Time*

(1996), *The Siege of Eternity* (1997), and *The Far Shore of Time* (1999) imagines the future Earth at the center of a galactic war. Pohl's numerous short-story collections include *The Best of Frederik Pohl* (1975), *Pohlstars* (1984), and *The Gateway Trip: Tales and Vignettes of the Heechee* (1990). Pohl also won Hugo Awards for best professional editor (1966–68), best short story (1973 and 1986), and best fan writer for his blog *The Way the Future Blogs* (2010).

In 1978 Pohl published a memoir, *The Way the Future Was*, and he collaborated with Asimov on an environmental handbook titled *Our Angry Earth* (1991). Pohl also wrote the biography *Tiberius* (1960), using the pseudonym Ernst Mason.

TERRY PRATCHETT

(b. 1948–)

E nglish author Terry Prachett writes predominantly humorous fantasy and fiction stories. He is best known for his *Discworld* series.

Terrence David John Pratchett was born in Beaconsfield, Buckinghamshire, Eng., on April 28, 1948. The son of an engineer and a

secretary, he was raised in Buckinghamshire. Pratchett became interested in science fiction and fantasy at a young age, publishing his first story, "The Hades Business," in a school magazine in 1961. The story was published commercially two years later in *Science Fantasy* magazine.

At age seventeen Pratchett left school in order to pursue a career in journalism. About this time he began working on his first novel, *The Carpet People*, which was published in 1971 (it was heavily revised and republished in 1992). The lighthearted tale, aimed at children, centers on the exploits of two brothers who live inside a carpet and battle the evil concept of Fray.

Pratchett continued to work in newspaper journalism and then in public relations throughout the 1970s and most of the '80s. He published two more stand-alone novels, *The Dark Side of the Sun* (1976) and *Strata* (1981), before the first book in his *Discworld* series, *The Colour of Magic*, was published in 1983. The series continued with *The Light Fantastic* (1986), *Equal Rites* (also 1986), and *Mort* (1987). The success of these books led Pratchett to quit his office job and become a full-time writer.

Pratchett's *Discworld* series, a collection of satirical fantasy novels set on a

disc-shaped world that rests on the backs of four giant elephants atop a humongous turtle, proved wildly popular worldwide, and he published one or more nearly every year into the early twenty-first century. The series also spawned video games, plays, television adaptations, and several supplemental volumes, including books of maps of the Discworld. While the bulk of the series was aimed at an adult audience, it was also popular with children; Pratchett penned several novels that were set on the Discworld and aimed specifically at a younger audience.

In addition to those set in the Discworld universe, Pratchett published several other novels for children, notably the *Bromeliad* trilogy (1989–90) and the *Johnny Maxwell* trilogy (1992–96). *Dodger* (2012) relays the adventures of a young man in Victorian London, where he encounters a Dickensian array of characters—among them Charles Dickens himself.

In 2007 Pratchett was diagnosed with a variant of early-onset Alzheimer's disease. He subsequently became an outspoken advocate for Alzheimer's research and awareness, donating $1 million to the cause and appearing in a 2009 BBC documentary about his life with the disease. Although his illness affected

his ability to read and write, Pratchett continued to regularly publish books. In 2010 he became an adjunct professor of English at the University of Dublin. Pratchett was the recipient of numerous honours and awards for his work; he was appointed an Officer in the Order of the British Empire in 1998 and was knighted in 2009.

PHILIP PULLMAN

(b. 1946–)

British author Philip Pullman wrote books for children, young adults, and adults. He is best known for the trilogy *His Dark Materials*, critically acclaimed, sophisticated fantasy books for young adults that have also proved popular with adults.

Philip Nicholas Pullman was born on October 19, 1946, in Norwich, Eng. His family moved many times during his childhood, as his father was an officer in the Royal Air Force. They settled for a time in Rhodesia (now Zimbabwe). After his father died in a plane crash, the young Pullman lived in England, Australia, and later Wales.

Philip Pullman, speaking at the Great Britons 2004 event in London upon receiving an award in the arts category. Gareth Cattermole/Getty Images

He studied English at the University of Oxford and then remained in the city of Oxford, working as a teacher.

Meanwhile, Pullman had begun writing novels. His first books, *The Haunted Storm* (1972) and *Galatea* (1976), were written for adults. Starting with *Count Karlstein, or Ride of the Demon Huntsman* (1982), Pullman began writing books for children and young adults. His Sally Lockhart detective stories, set in London during the Victorian era, were published between 1985 and 1994.

Pullman next wrote the *His Dark Materials* trilogy, which was greatly admired by readers and critics alike. It tells the story of Lyra Belacqua and Will Parry, who travel through parallel universes and grapple with fundamental questions of life and death. *Northern Lights*, the first volume, was published in England in 1995. It was later issued in the United States as *The Golden Compass*. The second part of the trilogy, *The Subtle Knife*, was published in 1997. The final part, *The Amber Spyglass*, appeared in 2000, becoming the first children's book to win the prestigious Whitbread Book of the Year Award (now the Costa Book of the Year Award), in 2001. Each book in the trilogy was also made into a BBC radio play, and the entire trilogy was adapted into two stage plays and performed at London's National Theater. The first book in the series was made into a major motion picture, *The Golden Compass*, in 2007.

Among Pullman's other works are *How to Be Cool* (1987), *The Broken Bridge* (1990), *The White Mercedes* (1992; reissued and filmed as *The Butterfly Tattoo* in 2009), *The Firework-Maker's Daughter* (1995), and *The Scarecrow and the Servant* (2004). His novel *The Good Man Jesus and the Scoundrel Christ* (2010) is a retelling of the Gospel stories in which Mary gives birth to twins: a healthy, charismatic son named Jesus and a sickly, introspective, and scholarly son called Christ.

J.K. ROWLING

(b. 1965–)

British author J.K. Rowling captured the imagination of children and adults alike with her best-selling series of books about Harry Potter, a young sorcerer in training. The books were critically acclaimed as well as wildly popular and were credited with generating a new interest in reading among children, the books' intended audience.

Joanne Kathleen Rowling was born on July 31, 1965, in Yate, near Bristol, Eng. She grew up in Chepstow, Gwent, Wales, where she wrote her first story at the age of six. After graduating from the University of Exeter in 1986, Rowling began working for Amnesty International in London. The idea for the Harry Potter stories came to her during a train ride in 1990, and she began writing the magic adventure while sitting in cafés and pubs.

In the early 1990s Rowling traveled to Portugal to teach English as a foreign language, but after a brief marriage and the birth of her daughter, she returned to the United Kingdom, settling in Edinburgh, Scotland. Living on public assistance between stints as a French teacher, she continued to write, often on scraps of paper and napkins.

After being rejected by several publishers, Rowling's first manuscript was purchased by Bloomsbury Children's Books in 1996. *Harry Potter and the Philosopher's Stone* (1997), which was known in the United States as *Harry Potter and the Sorcerer's Stone*, was an immediate success. The book received numerous awards, including the British Book Award. All six succeeding volumes—*Harry Potter and the Chamber of Secrets* (1998), *Harry Potter and*

J.K. Rowling, author of the popular Harry Potter *series, signing autographs outside a London theater during the European premiere of* Harry Potter and the Order of the Phoenix. Dave M. Benett/Getty Images

the Prisoner of Azkaban (1999), Harry Potter and the Goblet of Fire (2000), Harry Potter and the Order of the Phoenix (2003), Harry Potter and the Half-Blood Prince (2005), and Harry Potter and the Deathly Hallows (2007), which was the seventh and final book in the series—also were best-sellers, available in more than 200 countries and some 60 languages.

In 2001 the companion books Fantastic Beasts & Where to Find Them and Quidditch Through the Ages were published, with the proceeds going to charity. A movie based on the first Harry Potter book, released in November 2001, broke box-office records for its first-weekend gross in both the United Kingdom and North America. A series of film sequels followed. Rowling was appointed an Officer of the British Empire in 2001. In 2012, Rowling published her first novel for adults, The Casual Vacancy.

JOANNA RUSS

(b. 1937–d. 2011)

American writer Joanna Russ introduced a feminist twist to the traditionally male-dominated science fiction genre. Her most notable work was *The Female Man* (1975).

Joanna Ruth Russ was born in Bronx, N.Y., on Feb. 22, 1937. She earned a B.A. in English (1957) from Cornell University, Ithaca, N.Y., and an M.A. in playwriting and dramatic literature (1960) from Yale University.

Russ published her first story in 1959, and by the late 1960s she had scored notable successes with a series of stories featuring the time-hopping female adventurer Alyx, who was also the protagonist in her first novel, *Picnic on Paradise* (1968). *The Female Man* examines four women in distinctly different historical contexts.

In addition, Russ wrote essays, short fiction, and literary criticism. She died on April 29, 2011, in Tucson, Ariz.

CLIFFORD D. SIMAK

(b. 1904–d. 1988)

While his contemporaries were busy producing mainstream science fiction about interstellar battles with menacing alien races and nuclear holocausts,

Clifford D. Simak generally avoided elements of violence in his writing. By the end of his career he had perfected his own style—sometimes called "Simakian"—which was often grounded in rural or pastoral settings with underlying themes of individualism and compassion.

Simak was born on Aug. 3, 1904, in Millville, Wis., a rural farm town, which he used as the setting for many of his most notable works, including the novels *Way Station* (1963) and *All Flesh Is Grass* (1965). Though he was a prominent science fiction writer of his generation, having published numerous award-winning short stories and novels, he maintained a full-time career as a newspaperman for more than five decades.

His first published work of science fiction, the short story "The World of the Red Sun" (1939), was featured in *Wonder Stories* magazine. The story involved time travel, an element that he frequently revisited throughout his career. Often touted as his greatest achievement, *City* (1952), a collection of short stories written between 1944 and 1951, won the International Fantasy Award in 1953.

Way Station, which won the Hugo Award for best novel in 1964, was another example of Simak's fascination with rural settings and unlikely protagonists. In this case, his main character, a humble farmer, is given the gift of immortality by aliens in return for using his house as a portal to travel between planets.

Throughout his career, Simak occasionally ventured beyond science fiction, penning a handful of western short stories and non-fiction titles, including *The Solar System, Our New Front Yard* (1962). He won the Science Fiction Writers of America's Grand Master Award in 1977 and the Bram Stoker Award for lifetime achievement in 1987. He died on April 25, 1988, in Minneapolis, Minn., at the age of eighty-three.

E.E. SMITH

(b. 1890–d. 1965)

Author E.E. Smith is credited with creating the science fiction subgenre of "space opera." Tales in this subgenre are action-adventure stories set on a vast

intergalactic scale, typically involving faster-than-light spaceships, powerful weapons, and fantastic technology.

Edward Elmer Smith was born in Sheboygan, Wis., on May 2, 1890. He received a bachelor's degree in chemical engineering from the University of Idaho, Moscow, in 1914 and became a chemist at the U.S. Department of Agriculture in Washington, D.C. During 1915 Smith began writing what would become the novel *The Skylark of Space* with his neighbour, Lee Hawkins Garby, who wrote the romantic parts of the story that Smith felt he could not write. Smith continued to write while completing (1919) a doctoral degree in chemistry from George Washington University, Washington, D.C.

In 1919 Smith became a chemist at the milling company F.W. Stock and Sons in Hillsdale, Michigan, specializing in doughnut mixes. In 1920 Smith and Garby completed the novel; however, Smith was unable to find a publisher until 1928, when the novel was serialized in *Amazing Stories*.

Response to *The Skylark of Space* was extremely positive, and Smith immediately began work on a sequel, *Skylark Three* (1930). When it, too, was published in *Amazing Stories*, Smith was credited as Edward E. Smith, Ph.D., earning him the nickname among science fiction fans of "Doc" Smith. The series continued with *Skylark of Valeron* (1934–35) and *Skylark DuQuesne* (1965).

Smith originally conceived of his next series as a single gigantic novel, but it was published from 1937 to 1948 as four separate books in the *Lensman* series: *Galactic Patrol* (1937–38), *Gray Lensman* (1939–40), *Second Stage Lensmen* (1941–42), and *Children of the Lens* (1947–48). Smith penned two prequels to the *Lensman* books: *Triplanetary* (originally 1934; revised for the series in 1948) and *First Lensman* (1950). Another novel, *The Vortex Blaster* (1941–42; also called *Masters of the Vortex*), is set in the Lensman universe but does not follow the narrative threads of the other *Lensman* books.

Smith's works were criticized for having many of the faults of pulp writing, such as wooden dialogue and clichéd characters. However, his groundbreaking adventures, with their breathless action and cosmic scale, were an enormous influence on the science fiction that followed. Smith died on Aug. 31, 1965, in Seaside, Ore.

OLAF STAPLEDON

(b. 1886–d. 1950)

English author Olaf Stapledon wrote works of both philosophy and science fiction throughout his career. He is remembered primarily for his "histories of the future," which proved highly influential in the development of science fiction.

William Olaf Stapledon was born near Liverpool, Eng., on May 10, 1886. A pacifist, he served with a Friends' ambulance unit in World War I and was awarded the Croix de Guerre. He received a doctorate in philosophy and psychology from the University of Liverpool. In 1929 he published *A Modern Theory of Ethics* and seemed destined for an academic career, but after the success of his novel *Last and First Men* (1930), he began to write fiction.

Last and First Men traces the history of humanity from the First Men (present-day) to the Eighteenth Men, one of whom serves as narrator. The tale illustrates Stapledon's belief that to emphasize either the physical—represented by the flying Seventh Men of Venus—or the mental—represented by the giant-brained

Fourth Men—to the exclusion of the other spells certain disaster. Stapledon emphasized the ideals of community, necessary for individual fulfillment and embodied by the Eighteenth Men, and of spirit, which gives purpose to human existence. He used themes of antiquity and myths of the past to create a myth of the future.

Stapledon's nonfiction works include *Philosophy and Living* (1938) and *Beyond the "Isms"* (1942). He also wrote for technical and scholarly reviews on ethics and philosophy. His other works of fiction include *The Last Men in London* (1932), *Odd John* (1935), *Star Maker* (1937), and *Sirius* (1944). He died on Sept. 6, 1950, in Cheshire, Eng.

BRUCE STERLING

(b. 1954–)

I n the mid-1980s, a subgenre of science fiction known as cyberpunk emerged. These were stories in which the main characters were not heroes, but more likely outsiders trapped in a dehumanized, high-tech future. American science fiction

author Bruce Sterling was a major proponent of this type of storytelling, notably as the editor of *Mirrorshades: The Cyberpunk Anthology* (1986).

He was born Michael Bruce Sterling in Brownsville, Texas, on April 14, 1954. In 1976 Sterling graduated from the University of Texas at Austin and published his first story, "Man-Made Self," in the anthology *Lone Star Universe*. His first novel, *Involution Ocean* (1977), describes a planet where inhabitants escape their confusing lives through drug abuse. That was followed by *The Artificial Kid*, published in 1980. His novel *Schismatrix* (1985) and the short-story collection *Crystal Express* (1989) examine the contrasting lives of the Shapers, who changes their appearance through genetics, and the Mechanists, who use prosthetic devices to alter themselves.

Other fiction by Sterling includes *Islands in the Net* (1988), and *The Difference Engine* (1990) written with William Gibson. In 1992 Sterling published *Globalhead*, a volume of short fiction, and the nonfiction work *The Hacker Crackdown: Law and Disorder on the Electronic Frontier*, an exposé of computer crime. His later works include *Heavy Weather* (1994) and *Holy Fire* (1996).

Author Bruce Sterling addressing the crowd at the 2012 SXSW Music, Film + Interactive Festival in Austin, Texas. Mindy Best/WireImage/Getty Images

MARY STEWART

(b. 1916–)

British author Mary Stewart is best known for her update of Arthurian legend in a popular trilogy of novels about the magician Merlin. She also wrote suspense novels and books for children.

Mary Florence Elinor Stewart was born in Sunderland, Durham, Eng., on Sept. 17, 1916. She attended the University of Durham, obtaining a bachelor's degree in 1938 and a master's degree in 1941. During the 1940s and early 1950s she taught English literature at her alma mater, but she turned to writing full-time upon publication of her first novel, *Madam, Will You Talk?*, in 1955.

Stewart wrote nine more popular romantic thrillers before turning to historical fiction and legend in the late 1960s. The first novel of her *Merlin* trilogy, *The Crystal Cave*, appeared in 1970, followed by *The Hollow Hills* (1973) and *The Last Enchantment* (1979); all were well received by critics and the public. Stewart's fourth book based on Arthurian

legend, *The Wicked Day* (1983), presents King Arthur's traitorous nephew Mordred as a tragic figure rather than as pure villain.

Stewart also wrote books for children. These titles include *The Little Broomstick* (1971), *Ludo and the Star Horse* (1974), and *A Walk in Wolf Wood* (1980).

THEODORE STURGEON

(b. 1918–d. 1985)

American science fiction writer Theodore Sturgeon emphasized romantic and sexual themes in his stories. He is also known for writing several episodes of the classic sci-fi television series *Star Trek*.

Sturgeon was born Edward Hamilton Waldo; Theodore Sturges was one of his pseudonyms. After dropping out of high school, he worked at a variety of jobs. He sold his first short story in 1937 and began to publish in science fiction magazines

under various names. He was especially prolific between 1946 and 1958.

Sturgeon was unusual among his peers in writing about loneliness, love, and sex. His characters typically are young and repressed, saved from their isolation with the help of superhuman forces or by the development of special powers. His stories are considered daring for featuring the problems of hermaphrodites (people with both male and female sex organs), exiled lovers, and homosexuals.

Arguably his most famous work is the novel *More than Human* (1953), about six outcast children with extrasensory powers. He followed that with *Venus plus X* (1960), which details a "perfect world" achieved by the elimination of all sexual differences. Sturgeon's other science fiction and fantasy novels include *The Dreaming Jewels* (1950; also published as *The Synthetic Man*), *The Cosmic Rape* (1958), and *Some of Your Blood* (1961).

Sturgeon also wrote western, historical, and mystery novels and television scripts. including several for the *Star Trek* series; he was the formulator of the series' Prime Directive, a policy of noninterference with other cultures. Sturgeon also worked as a columnist for the magazine *National Review.* He died in Eugene, Ore., on May 8, 1985.

J.R.R. TOLKIEN

(b. 1892–d. 1973)

H is heroes are rather short, rather stout, and have very furry feet. English author J.R.R. Tolkien's fantastic tales of battles between good and evil, including *The Lord of the Rings trilogy*, made "hobbit" a household word.

John Ronald Reuel Tolkien was born in Bloemfontein, South Africa, on Jan. 3, 1892, and moved at age four with his family to England, where he was educated at Exeter College, Oxford. He was a professor at Oxford from 1925 to 1959 and first gained recognition as a philologist, a person who studies the way language is used in literature. This work led him to help edit a version of the English fable *Sir Gawain and the Green Knight* that was published in 1925.

Tolkien not only studied fables; he created new ones of his own. He invented an

Portrait of novelist J.R.R. Tolkien, who wrote the popular and beloved Lord of the Rings *trilogy.*
Mondadori/Getty Images

imaginary land, Middle Earth, in meticulous detail: its language, its geography, and its exciting history. *The Hobbit: Or, There and Back Again*, published in 1937, introduces readers to this special world as its inhabitants—elves, dwarfs, wizards, and the furry-footed hobbit Bilbo Baggins—fight and win against an evil dragon.

This story is continued in *The Lord of the Rings* trilogy (1954–55), consisting of *The Fellowship of the Ring, The Two Towers,* and *The Return of the King.* These tales became immensely popular in the 1960s, especially among young adults. Another Tolkien book on Middle Earth, *The Silmarillion*, was published four years after his death in Bournemouth, Eng., on Sept. 2, 1973.

JACK VANCE

(b. 1916–d. 2013)

American author Jack Vance was an influential mystery, fantasy, and science fiction writer whose career spanned more than six decades. Over the course of his career, he published sixty full-length

titles and numerous short stories under several pseudonyms, including Alan Wade and Peter Held, which showcased his ability to craft colorful characters and the worlds they inhabit.

John Holbrook Vance was born in San Francisco, Calif., on Aug. 28, 1916. He spent most of his life in and around the region. It was in the 1940s that Vance decided to pursue a career as a professional writer.

Throughout the 1940s and 1950s, Vance sold numerous science fiction short stories to pulp magazines. His first published piece was "The World-Thinker" (1945), which appeared in *Thrilling Wonder Stories*. His first financial success in writing came when Twentieth Century-Fox hired him as a screenwriter for the television series *Captain Video* (1949).

By the end of the 1950s Vance had written several mystery novels and published the influential collection of science fiction short stories *Dying Earth* (1950). The 1960s, however, saw the publication of his most critically acclaimed works, including *The Man in the Cage* (1961), for which he won an Edgar Award for best first mystery novel. Additionally, *The Dragon Masters* (1962) won him the Hugo

Award for short fiction, and *The Last Castle* (1967) won both the Nebula and Hugo awards.

Vance often incorporated elements of mystery and crime thrillers into his science fiction novels, including *Son of the Tree* (1951), *Marune: Alastor 933* (1975), and *The Book of Dreams* (1981). His short stories about an interstellar detective named Magnus Ridolph were anthologized in *The Complete Magnus Ridolph* (1985).

Vance was presented with the World Fantasy Award for lifetime achievement in 1984 and the Science Fiction Writers of America's Grand Master Award in 1997. He was inducted into the Science Fiction Hall of Fame in 2001. His memoir *This Is Me, Jack Vance! (or, More Properly, This Is "I")* (2009) earned him his third Hugo Award. Vance died at his home in Oakland, Calif., on May 26, 2013.

A.E. VAN VOGT

(b. 1912–d. 2000)

Canadian science fiction author A.E. van Vogt emerged as one of the leading

writers of the genre in the mid-twentieth century. His stories are characterized as fast-paced adventures with complex, sometimes confusing plots.

Alfred Elton van Vogt was born in Winnipeg, Manitoba, Canada, on April 26, 1912. He attended the University of Ottawa and began his writing career in the early 1930s, selling fictional articles to confession magazines. After writing a number of radio plays, he turned to science fiction. His first published story in the genre, "Black Destroyer," appeared in the July 1939 issue of *Astounding Science Fiction*, which at the time was considered the leading science fiction magazine; he thereafter became a regular contributor.

Van Vogt's first novel, *Slan* (1946; serialized in *Astounding Science Fiction*, September to December 1940) told the story of mutants with superhuman powers. It was followed by one of van Vogt's classics, *The Weapon Makers* (1947), first serialized in 1943. Other works first serialized in the 1940s were *The World of A* (1948; later published as *The World of Null-A*), a mysterious story about a developing superhero, and *The Weapon Shops of Isher* (1951), a sequel to *The Weapon Makers*.

Van Vogt, who moved to the United States in 1944, took a break from science fiction writing in the 1950s to help develop Dianetics, which was later incorporated into Scientology. He resumed his writing career in the 1960s but was unable to achieve his earlier level of success. His later novels include *The Silkie* (1969), *Renaissance* (1979), and *The Cosmic Encounter* (1980).

Van Vogt died in Los Angeles, Calif., on Jan. 26, 2000. The cause of death was listed as pneumonia.

JULES VERNE

(b. 1828–d. 1905)

The startling inventions described in the novels of Jules Verne seemed highly fantastic to the readers of his time. Today he is regarded as a prophet. His dreams of undersea and air travel have come true, and Verne's story *Around the World in Eighty Days* now seems a record of a leisurely trip.

Jules Verne was born on February 8, 1828, in Nantes, France. With his brother, young Jules sailed on the Loire River, often going down to the sea. To the boy's active

imagination the leaky boat was a palatial yacht and every scene an important geographic discovery. His father was a lawyer and wanted Jules to follow the same profession. When Jules was sent to school in Paris, however, he studied literature instead of law.

Verne began to write poetry and plays at an early age, but he had little success until he published *Five Weeks in a Balloon* in 1863. This fantastic tale delighted readers, both young and old. Its success led Verne to continue writing exciting stories of adventure. He studied geography and science to get ideas for his tales.

Verne's works include many short stories and more than fifty novels. The most popular novels include *A Journey to the Center of the Earth* (1864), *From the Earth to the Moon* (1865), *The Mysterious Island* (1870), *Twenty Thousand Leagues Under the Sea* (1870), and *Around the World in Eighty Days* (1872).

Verne's influence extends beyond literature and film into the world of science and technology, where he inspired generations of scientists, inventors, and explorers. In 1954 the United States Navy launched the world's first nuclear-powered submarine, named for Verne's *Nautilus*. Verne died on March 24, 1905, in Amiens, France.

French author Jules Verne, many of whose fantastical stories turned out to be prophetic. Boyer/H. Roger-Viollet

H.G. WELLS

(b. 1866–d. 1946)

A broken leg is not likely to start a boy on a career as a popular author, but it did so for young H.G. Wells. As he lay in bed he discovered a fascinating world of books.

Herbert George Wells was born in Bromley, in Kent, Eng. After grammar school he won a scholarship to the Normal School of Science in London. Later he earned a bachelor of science degree with honors. He wanted to be a science teacher. Tuberculosis made this impossible, so he turned to writing.

From his science training he drew a long series of novels, including *The Time Machine* (1895), *The War of the Worlds* (1898), *The Island of Dr. Moreau* (1896), *The Invisible Man* (1897), *The First Men in the Moon* (1901), and *The Shape of Things to Come* (1933). Reflecting his lower-middle-class background were *Kipps* (1905), *Tono-Bungay* (1909), and *The History of Mr. Polly* (1910). His most famous nonfiction works are *The Outline of History* (1920) and

An education in science and a love of literature combined to build the career of British storyteller H.G. Wells. Karsh/Woodfin Camp and Associates

The Science of Life (1929). Altogether, Wells wrote more than one hundred books.

The failure of statesmen to secure a lasting peace after World War I impelled Wells into awakening mankind to the instability of the world order. He wrote *The Outline of History* and *The Work, Wealth and Happiness of Mankind* (1932) in this period. He also interviewed Joseph Stalin and Franklin D. Roosevelt in an attempt to resolve the conflict between Communism and capitalism.

Except for brief periods on the Riviera, Wells lived in London for most of his life. He was married twice and had two sons by his second wife. His older son, George, a scientist, worked with him and Julian Huxley on *The Science of Life.* Wells died on Aug. 13, 1946.

T.H. WHITE

(b. 1906–d. 1964)

E nglish author, social historian, and satirist T.H. White was best known for a quartet of fantasy novels collectively

known as *The Once and Future King*, an adaptation of Sir Thomas Malory's fifteenth-century romance *Le Morte d'Arthur.* White had great knowledge of medieval customs, and his adaptation brought Britain's traditional saga of King Arthur to audiences around the world.

Terence Hanbury White was born in Bombay, India, on May 29, 1906, to Constance and Garrick White. His father was a policeman, and the family moved to England in 1911. His childhood was unhappy except for a brief period when he lived with his maternal grandparents. His parents divorced when he was fourteen. He studied at Cheltenham College and at Queens' College in Cambridge, from which he graduated in 1928. He taught at an English preparatory school and then at the Stowe School in Buckinghamshire from 1930 to 1936.

While teaching, he wrote an autobiographical work, *England Have My Bones* (1936), which attained critical success. Later he devoted himself exclusively to writing and to studying Arthurian legend and other subjects. White was by nature a recluse who often isolated himself

from human society and spent his time hunting, fishing, and looking after his collection of pets. After 1946 he lived in the Channel Islands.

His other works include *Mistress Masham's Repose* (1946); *The Goshawk* (1951), which was a study of falconry; *The Scandalmonger* (1951), a work of social history; *The Book of Beasts* (1954); and *The Master* (1957). *The Once and Future King* (1958) comprises *The Sword in the Stone* (1939); *The Queen of Air and Darkness*, which was first published as *The Witch in the Wood* (1940); *The Ill-Made Knight* (1941); and *The Candle in the Wind.* Years after White's death, *The Book of Merlyn* (1977) was published as a conclusion to *The Once and Future King* based on a manuscript of White's discovered by the University of Texas Press.

The Once and Future King was adapted by Alan Jay Lerner and Frederick Loewe in 1960 into a highly successful musical play, *Camelot*, which in turn was made into a motion picture in 1967. White died on Jan. 17, 1964, aboard the S.S. *Exeter* near Piraeus, Greece, where he was traveling after an American speaking tour.

JACK WILLIAMSON

(b. 1908–d. 2006)

A merican science fiction writer Jack
Williamson produced more than fifty
books during his career. To many he is second
only to Robert Heinlein as the leading author‑
ity and producer of science fiction literature.

John Stewart Williamson was born in
Bisbee, a town in the territory that has
now become the state of Arizona, on April
29, 1908. His first story, "The Metal Man,"
appeared in 1928 in the magazine *Amazing
Stories*, but it was his novel *The Humanoids*
(1949), a cautionary tale about the danger
of too much human reliance on technol‑
ogy, especially robots, that became his most
famous. Another novel, *Darker than You Think*
(1948), a horror story about werewolves, also
became a classic. He teamed with Frederik
Pohl to write a number of books, including
the compelling *Starchild* trilogy (1964–69).

Williamson received the Nebula
Grand Master Award in 1975 and was the
recipient of the 1994 World Fantasy Life
Achievement Award. He was inducted
into the Science Fiction Hall of Fame in

1996. Williamson died on Nov. 10, 2006, in Portales, New Mexico.

ROGER ZELAZNY

(b. 1937–d. 1995)

U.S. science fiction writer Roger Zelazny was best known for his the *Chronicles of Amber* series. He was a three-time Nebula Award winner and won the coveted Hugo Award six times.

Robert Joseph Zelazny was born on May 13, 1937, in Cleveland, Ohio. He first became prominent in the 1960s as one of the best of the "new wave." Rather than optimistically celebrating new technologies as the earlier generation of science fiction writers had, his works explored the implications for humanity of the changes that technology had brought to the twentieth century.

The *Chronicles of Amber* series consists of ten books published from 1970 to 1997, that are divided into two subseries of five books each. An interactive computer game based on the first book in the series, *Nine Princes in Amber*, was released in 1987; the full series also inspired a role-playing game.

Though Zelazny was the winner of many awards for such books as *Lord of Light* (1967) and *Eye of Cat* (1982), his later books were less successful with critics and the public than his early works. He died on June 14, 1995, in Santa Fe, New Mexico.

PAUL ZINDEL

(b. 1936–d. 2003)

U.S. playwright and author Paul Zindel was born on May 15, 1936, on Staten Island, N.Y. His plays and novels combined elements of fantasy, science fiction, and humor to create a highly individualized style.

Zindel attended Wagner College, from which he received a bachelor's degree in 1958 and a master's degree the following year. He taught high school chemistry for ten years before turning to writing plays and children's books. His play *The Effect of Gamma Rays on Man-in-the-Moon Marigolds* (1964) won several awards, including an Obie Award and a Pulitzer Prize for drama. It told the story of two sisters and their overbearing mother. Parents and

adolescents alike found the play appealing and unerring in its view of young adulthood.

Zindel's novels included *The Pigman* (1968), *My Darling, My Hamburger* (1969), *Pardon Me, You're Stepping on My Eyeball* (1974), *I Love My Mother* (1975), *The Undertaker's Gone Bananas!* (1979), and *The Girl Who Wanted a Boy* (1982). These were written for an audience of young adults.

Zindel was criticized for a moralizing tone that was evident in several of his books, but he received praise for accurately reproducing the nuances of youthful dialogue. Zindel's other plays included *And Miss Reardon Drinks a Little* (1971), *Let Me Hear You Whisper: A Play* (1974), and *Ladies at the Alamo* (1975). Several of his works were adapted for television and motion pictures. Zindel died in New York City on March 27, 2003.

Glossary

anthology A collection of selected works of literature.

apocalyptic Relating to or about the end of the world.

chide To angrily express disapproval.

cyberpunk A form of science fiction dealing with future urban societies dominated by computer technology.

genre A category of artistic composition, including literature, characterized by a particular form or style.

illusory Stemming from a misleading image; something that is not what it appears to be.

induct To admit as a member.

obsessive Excessive, often to an unreasonable degree.

parody A literary or musical work in which the style of an author or work is closely imitated for comic effect or in ridicule.

prolific Abundantly productive.

protagonist The main character in a literary work.

pseudonym A fictitious name; when used by a writer, also called a pen name.

pulp magazine A genre-specific magazine
printed on poor-quality (or pulp) paper
that made it inexpensive, and therefore
easily purchased by the general public.

satirize To make fun of human flaws and
shortcomings in a clever, witty way
through a work of literature or art.

utopia An imaginary or remote location
or state of being where life is perfect
all the time.

For More Information

Gunn Center for the Study of Science Fiction
University of Kansas
1445 Jayhawk Boulevard
3001 Wescoe Hall
Lawrence, KS 66045
Web site: http://www.sfcenter.ku.edu
The Gunn Center for the Study of Science Fiction offers programs, workshops, online courses, and news about the genre to teachers, sci-fi readers, and the general public. Each year the center conducts an intensive institute on a particular form of science fiction, such as short stories.

Merril Collection of Science Fiction, Speculation and Fantasy
Toronto Public Library – Lillian H. Smith Branch
239 College Street
Toronto, ON M5T 1R5
Canada
(416) 393-7748

Web site: http://www.torontopubliclibrary.
ca/merril

The Merril Collection of Science Fiction,
Speculation and Fantasy maintains a
catalog of more than 72,000 books,
periodicals, manuscripts, and other
materials related to the science fiction
and fantasy genres. The organization
also hosts events, and displays science
fiction–related exhibits and artwork on
premises.

MIT Science Fiction Society

W 20-473

84 Massachusetts Avenue

Cambridge, MA 02139

(617) 258-5126

Web site: http://mitsfs.mit.edu

The MIT Science Fiction Society maintains a large, open-shelf science fiction
collection, with a complete searchable
database. The society also hosts weekly
meetings and publishes creative content
and reviews by members.

National Fantasy Fan Federation (N3F)

P.O. Box 1925

Mountain View, CA 94041

Web site: http://n3f.org

The National Fantasy Fan Federation, more commonly known as N3F, offers writing workshops, online and "snail mail" discussion groups, pen-pal connections, conventions, and reviews of science fiction and fantasy literature.

Northwest Science Fiction Society (NWSFS)

P.O. Box 24207

Seattle, WA 98124

(425) 686-9737

Web site: http://nwsfs.com

The NWSFS is a forum for science fiction fans throughout the northwest United States and Canada. Meetings, discussion groups, and a newsletter are a few of the organization's offerings.

Science Fiction Research Association (SFRA)

3854 Del Mar Avenue

Loomis, CA 95650

Web site: http://www.sfra.org

Founded in 1970, the Science Fiction Research Association is dedicated to the study of science fiction and fantasy

across media. The organization offers publications, conferences, teaching aids, and information about notable achievements in the field.

Web Sites

Due to the changing nature of Internet links, Rosen Educational Services has developed an online list of Web sites related to the subject of this book. This site is updated regularly. Please use this link to access the list:

http://www.rosenlinks.com/eafct/scifi

For Further Reading

Abrams, Dennis. *H.G. Wells.* New York, NY:
    Facts On File, 2011.
Belviso, Meg, and Pamela Pollock. *Who Is
    J.K. Rowling?* New York, NY: Grosset &
    Dunlap, 2012.
Butcher, William. *Jules Verne: The Definitive
    Biography.* New York, NY: Thunder's
    Mouth, 2006.
Duriez, Colin. *Tolkien and C.S. Lewis:
    The Gift of Friendship.* Mahwah, NJ:
    Paulist, 2003.
Heaphy, Maura. *Science Fiction Authors: A
    Research Guide.* Westport, CT: Libraries
    Unlimited, 2008.
Martin, Philip. *A Guide to Fantasy
    Literature: Thoughts on Stories of Wonder
    and Enchantment.* Milwaukee, WI:
    Crickhollow Books, 2009.
Miller, Ron. *The History of Science Fiction.*
    Danbury, CT: Scholastic, 2001.
Piddock, Charles. *Ray Bradbury: Legendary
    Fantasy Writer.* New York, NY: Gareth
    Stevens, 2009.

Seed, David. *Science Fiction: A Very Short Introduction.* Oxford, England: University of Oxford Press, 2011.

Stevens, Jennifer, and Dorothea Salo. *Fantasy Authors: A Research Guide.* Westport, CT: Libraries Unlimited, 2008.

Index